THE CANE TOAD REPUBLIC

D1799386

David Flint was educated at the universities of Sydney, London and Paris. He is an Emeritus Professor of Law and Chairman of the Australian Broadcasting Authority and the World Association of Press Councils. He was Chairman of the Australian Press Council between 1987 and 1997, and has published widely on topics such as the media, international economic law and Australia's constitution. David Flint is a Member of the Order of Australia, 1995, and received the World Outstanding Legal Scholar award, World Jurists Association, 1991. He lives in Sydney, and is National Convenor of Australians for Constitutional Monarchy.

THE CANE TOAD REPUBLIC

DAVID FLINT

**Wakefield
Press**

Wakefield Press
Box 2266
Kent Town
South Australia 5071

First published 1999

Designed and typeset by Clinton Ellicott
Printed and bound by Hyde Park Press, Adelaide

National Library of Australia
Cataloguing-in-publication entry

Flint, David (David Edward), 1938–   .

Bibliography.
ISBN 1 86254 496 4.

1. Republicanism – Australia. 2. Republicanism – Australia – History.
3. Monarchy – Australia. 4. Heads of state – Australia.
5. Federal government – Australia. 6. Constitutional law – Australia.
7. Australia – Politics and government. I. Title.

321.80994

CONTENTS

FOREWORD

by Christopher Pearson

One of the fascinating things about the supporters of Australia's version of a constitutional monarchy is the diversity of routes by which they arrived at their positions. Another is the role that civil liberty played in their thinking. Justice Michael Kirby, a founding convener of Australians for Constitutional Monarchy, supports the monarchy among other reasons because it protected the liberty of a Communist grandparent. David Flint reached a similar view in part because of the freedom it accorded to his grandparents when they emigrated from the Dutch East Indies. His analysis of Australian institutions under fire from the *Bulletin* around Federation ("the anti-racist crown attacked by the racist republican press" is how he summarises it) is particularly thought-provoking.

The practical emphasis on liberty and the actual experience of marginalisation is in pronounced contrast to the modish preoccupations of the corporatist push behind the Keating–Turnbull model. The best arguments the latter can muster rely on symbolism, theoretical abstractions and the failings of the House of Windsor. Instead David Flint poses the fundamental question: In what ways would republican change enhance or further protect our freedom?

The answer is, of course, none at all. Rather, because of its increasingly apparent structural problems, the model is unsafe and potentially catastrophic. One of the admirable things David Flint has achieved in this book is to argue those propositions from a variety of perspectives. He gives good republican reasons, a good sceptical and a libertarian case, as well as the monarchist point of view on why "this is the most ill-considered and dangerous proposal ever put to the Australian people in a referendum".

The Cane Toad Republic distinguishes itself from other previous works on the subject by the amount of propaganda and popular misconceptions that it disposes of once and for all. It will be a brave republican, no matter how eminent, who attempts to rely on the notion of "an Australian head of state" as a reason for change. It was only ever a rhetorical ploy, because the distinction between a sovereign and a constitutional head of state – in our case the governor-general – has been well understood as a matter of both law and practice since long before Federation.

Another misconception to fall by the wayside is that Gough Whitlam shares the republicans' feigned confusion over the vice-regal role: "some people seem to think that it is an extraordinary concept but constitutionally it is quite obvious. He is the stand-in for the Queen when she is not in residence here. He can do everything that she can do as head of state. The system of governor-general works quite well. After all, no government of any political complexion can be better pleased than with a system where the head of state, the ceremonial head, holds the position for a certain number of years on the nomination of the national head of government."

Gough Whitlam's grasp of history reminds us of Paul Keating's lack of it. As Professor Flint points out: "On more than one occasion Keating claimed the constitution was drafted in and imposed by the British Foreign Office. His listeners' immediate reaction must have been that surely he meant the Colonial Office. In any event the prime minister was soon reminded that our constitution was in fact drafted in Australia, by Australians. And unlike the US or Canada, our constitution was actually approved by the Australian people in each of the states, not just by politicians."

A livelier appreciation of the constitution as a home-grown, distinctively Australian achievement should help counteract the trivialising deprecation of it by Jim McClelland and others as "a horse-and-buggy arrangement". As David Flint notes, no American says that about their constitution "although it still bears the stamp of a slave-owning society. Yet theirs is twice as old."

History should inform our understanding of the constitutional framework that has helped us become one of the freest, most stable and prosperous of democracies. But this book is about practical problems for the immediate future. It is a sure bet that the people who so blithely accept that the Keating–Turnbull republic is timely and proof of our collective maturity haven't confronted the sort of hard-headed argument it has to offer.

How many who are thinking of voting "yes" understand that this proposal is a politicians' republic which will consolidate their hold on power? How many know that the president would have no constitutional auditor's role, if the referendum passes, despite the fact that such a drastic curtailing of power was not contemplated at the Constitutional Convention?

It is not yet widely understood that the presidential powers, largely undefined, could be subject to judicial review for the first time by the high court – notwithstanding a last-minute amendment. As David Flint in his capacity as a professor of law points out, any crisis involving their exercise could drag on for months. As well, the reserve powers would be undermined by their becoming justiciable and there is the other new problem of a prescribed presidential obligation to act on ministerial advice, even if the advice itself is illegal, improper or foolish.

If that forfeiture of an umpire's discretion sounds like a mare's nest, there is other abundant evidence that the model has been hastily conceived and ill-considered. David Flint's explanation of the role of deputy presidents (there may be more than one at a time) and the serial sackability of acting presidents drawn either from the ranks of governors or available deputies is particularly disquieting and instructive.

This is a pragmatist's account of an unsatisfactory proposal but it is also an accessible version of how the existing system actually works and why. It is not a sentimental account but a fleshing-out of why the constitution is so serviceable and how it is that, in Justice Michael Kirby's phrase, the crown has functioned to temper narrow nationalism and to soften brutal majoritarianism.

PREFACE

"You're not a republican?" I am sometimes asked. "Why not?" Not just because my grandparents and my mother came in the early days of Federation from what is now Indonesia, then the Dutch East Indies, to what was then one of the world's most advanced democracies. Certainly not because of my age. And not only because I have sworn an oath of allegiance.

The fundamental reason I am not a republican is that my study of, and experience in many other countries has confirmed that we in Australia are blessed with our present constitutional and political arrangements. We are one of a select group of seven countries that enjoy a long and unbroken tradition as a democracy. And five of these are constitutional monarchies. Elizabeth II is queen of four!

Republicanism is not part of our tradition. It is alien to Australia. It has nothing to do with our history or our culture. In the later nineteenth century an almost insignificant republican movement was associated with extreme racism. Nevertheless, there was a move at federation to have the governor-general elected. The founders of this nation rejected that. They knew the Westminster system makes government more accountable, and they did not want a presidential figure competing with parliament. We often hear our federal constitution described in disparaging terms as a "horse and buggy" constitution. No American does that with theirs, although it still bears the stamp of a slave owning society. Yet theirs is twice as old.

Our federal constitution was a remarkable achievement. In a few years our founders drafted a constitution that met with the approval of the people in each of the states. They arranged for referendums, and then for the British parliament to legislate. And they had no computers, faxes or aeroplanes! Achieving our "indissoluble federal commonwealth under the crown" was also remarkable for another reason. As founders John Quick and Robert Garran wrote, never before had a group of self-governing communities, without external pressure of any kind, deliberately chosen of their own free will to unite. Why? Because they had a "simple and intellectual conviction of the folly of disunion and the advantages of nationhood".

The crown is in fact central not only to our constitution but also to our history and development. It is important not so much because of the high standing and impeccable behaviour of the current sovereign, but because of the power it denies others. If you remove the crown from the constitution, its powers should go to the people for whom the crown is trustee.

And if Australians were to choose to become a republic, *they* certainly would not want the one proposed now, in which – as republicans themselves warn us – absolute or excessive executive power is given to the prime minister. The second Keating–Turnbull republic, scrambled together only to secure a majority of votes in the last days of the Constitutional Convention, would be the only republic in the world where the president – the constitutional umpire and auditor – holds office at the whim of the prime minister. This is the most ill considered and dangerous proposal ever put to the Australian people in a referendum.

Because this book dares to go behind the glib argument that the proposed change is only symbolic, and examines the details of the Keating–Turnbull republic, it will be greeted with howls of rage. It will be said to be part of the "mother of all scare campaigns". In reply, I would say to any such critics that the true test of this republic is this: Is it, if not better than, at least as good as our present constitution? The answer to anyone with an open mind is obvious.

The Australian Republican Movement and its supporters do not claim that their republic will improve the constitution or make it more democratic. Nor can they point to any real problem with the queen, the governor-general or the governors.

In the 1930s, Australia had a problem. Our sugar cane crop was being destroyed by the Greyback Beetle. The authorities decided to release a sackload of the Hawaiian Bufo Marinus into the canefields. They would deal with the Greyback Beetle.

The solution was not well thought out. It was worse than the problem. You see, Bufo liked Queensland. It ate everything – except the Greyback Beetle. Why? The Greyback Beetle can fly. And Bufo can't.

This was the beginning of the cane toad disaster.

Today, we don't even have a problem. Yet, we are told we must give up our constitutional system which works, and works well.

The Keating–Turnbull republic is, in reality, a Cane Toad republic.

David Flint, Sydney, 1999

AUTHOR'S NOTE

I should like to thank my researcher Damien Freeman for the valuable assistance he has given me; Melanie Parker, my personal assistant, for so managing my professional life that I could preserve some of my private time to complete this book; and the Honourable Mr Justice Lloyd Waddy who was the first Convenor of Australians for Constitutional Monarchy, the Hon. Tony Abbott, his successor Kerry Jones, as well as Natasha Clyne and the other staff and the many supporters of ACM, for their encouragement, and for their loyalty to the Australian crown and the Australian constitution.

1
AUSTRALIAN REPUBLICANISM – THE ORIGINS

There are two distinct approaches to constitutional reform, observes Professor Kenneth Minogue of the London School of Economics. One is evolutionary and minimalist, the other is theoretical, abstract, and often revolutionary.

The first recognises that when an evident evil arises in government, it needs to be corrected with as little disturbance as possible. This is the traditional Australian approach, as demonstrated not only in the way we have made our constitutions, but also in the way we change them. It could be summed up by the maxim, *Si fractrum non sit noli id reficere*, which could be translated as, "If it ain't broke, don't fix it." This is not a desire to cling to the past, but to preserve a system that has exhibited enough inner dynamism to survive the twentieth century. Minogue says that it is precisely that capacity of constitutional monarchy not just to change, but to respond continuously to changes in society itself, which is important.

But it is the theoretical and abstract approach that has dominated schools of political theory. It attempts to graft onto political reality some abstract concept. This is usually claimed to offer a supposedly logical solution to the problem of what ought to be done in the name of justice, democracy or equality.

In this process history is forgotten as the rationalist gets to work sharpening and applying his criteria. As Minogue observes, "Kant famously said that of mankind's crooked timber, nothing straight would ever be made. The rationalist gets out his incline plane and tries to straighten knots and smooth away rough patches, and if he is not careful, nothing authentic will be left."

This approach permeates radical political thought. The revolutionary French and Russian regimes are extreme examples of the use of the abstract precepts of democracy and equity. Regrettably, some say inevitably, they were translated in practice into awful regimes.

The Australian republicanism of Paul Keating, Malcolm Turnbull and the Australian Republican Movement is a softer version of this approach. An abstract concept – *the* republic – has become an obsession. When the republic, as an abstract notion, was turned into an actual model in 1998, and even supporters concluded that the model was worse than the "problem", we were told to ignore this. We are told to concentrate on *the* republic, and avert our eyes from *this* republic. So Leader of the Opposition Kim Beazley tells us that he will become "terribly depressed" if the referendum debate becomes one about the details of the model.

The word "republic", as with the term "head of state" is now so imprecise that it is used to describe all manner of different regimes. So the details *are* important.

The republicanism of previous centuries has little to do with the present push for an Australian republic. Indeed some of the ideas of earlier republicans are more consistent with the arguments of contemporary constitutional monarchists. That great eighteenth-century prophet of enlightened liberal government, Jean Jacques Rousseau, would have declared Australia, throughout its 100 years, an ideal republic. He would have come to the same conclusion about the six colonies, at least once they had been allowed self-government. "What I call a republic," wrote Rousseau, "is any state under the rule of law, whatever its form of government."

Another great French prophet and observer, Baron Charles de Montesquieu, found in the Westminster system something close to his republican ideal – the separation of powers, the rule of law and political liberty. Indeed, since the early part of the nineteenth century, when the Australian colonists sought to establish the institutions of responsible government on this continent, Australians have embraced what are broadly understood to be republican doctrines. That is why Australia can properly be called a "crowned republic".

So republicanism does not necessarily exclude constitutional monarchy.

Indeed republicanism has meant many things. It has not necessarily meant rule by the people. The ARM uses the word to indicate the absence of a constitutional monarch. And the ARM model excludes the popular election of a president. In its latest version it involves the appointment by a two-thirds majority of parliament of a president nominated by the prime minister. The president would hold office for a term of five years but at the pleasure of the prime minister.

As political scientist Graham Maddox argues, the ARM brand of republicanism has no roots in Australia's past or her traditions. He says our tradition is more linked to collective action and public ownership than rational economics would allow. Indeed, he suggests, those modern States with the strongest commitment to communal welfare are precisely those that have retained a constitutional monarchy: the Scandinavian States, the Netherlands, Belgium, the United Kingdom, Canada and, of course, Australia. As Jack Lang, a leading French socialist says, "I notice that the constitutional monarchies are the most democratic countries of Europe. I don't understand how there could be any debate about it."

There are traces of what could be called republicanism in the early days of European settlement in Australia. Indeed, before the turn of the eighteenth century, Australian republicans had this first martyr. Historian Mark McKenna tells the story of how Lieutenant McKeller had accused Mr John Boston, a republican, of publicly drinking to the murder of the king and to the annihilation of the constitution. Republican excess, he said, had been carefully and industriously inculcated into every part of the Boston household. This included Boston's pig, which had destroyed the property of one Captain Foveaux. So Lieutenant McKellar shot Boston's pig. Republicans can therefore mourn their first martyr to the cause – John Boston's republican pig! (McKenna, 14)

Colonial thinkers came to be divided as to how they understood republicanism. While some associated republicanism with nationalism, for many others republican aspirations meant no more than achieving constitutional and democratic governance by the people. To both, constitutional monarchy, or its absence, was a secondary issue.

With the coming of responsible government in the colonies by the middle of the last century, and with federation, most of the ambitions of both brands of nineteenth-century republicanism had been achieved. As Mark Twain noted in 1897, the country governed itself. So nationalist republican sentiment disappeared by the end of the century, remaining dormant until individuals in the intelligentsia and arts community revived it in the 1960s and 1970s. There was increased interest after the constitutional crisis of November 1975, much of it ill-informed. Thus Robert Hughes bases his republicanism on the belief that the queen has a power to dismiss the prime minister, a power she clearly disavowed in 1975. In this Hughes is completely wrong. The power to dismiss the prime minister is vested in, and only in, the governor-general. Changing to a republic would not in itself remove this power.

Interest in the republican cause gradually waned as the events of 1975 receded from view. It was not until the final decade of this century, with the Sydney 2000 Olympics and the centenary of federation in sight, that interest really consolidated in the debate about a republic. But this would have remained a subject for dinner party debate in the republican salons of Sydney and Melbourne but for the emergence of Paul Keating as prime minister. In 1993 Keating endorsed a school of official republicanism, the standard bearer of which remains the Australian Republican Movement.

The ARM's concept of official republicanism is an extremely narrow one. While it loudly proclaims its patriotism, its agenda is limited to one thing – removing the crown. Getting rid of the queen at any price.

At the Constitutional Convention of February 1998, ARM delegates, one after the other, related their stories of their particular conversions: how at some past time the republican truth dawned on them. But their appeals to patriotism have a strict agenda. It is one of only a symbolic political change.

In contrast with old Australian republicanism, many of the official republicans, and especially its leadership, are closely identified with the politics of globalisation: the opening of Australia to international markets, free trade, the free movement of money, and substantial, if not unlimited, foreign investment. Anthony Wedgewood Benn – a British republican and Labor politician – sees a parallel development in Britain. Just as the old empire was supported by bankers and others when it brought a profit, the monarchy will be ditched, he says, when it is no longer useful. If its networks of oaths of allegiance and sovereignty interfere with profit-making in the new Europe, the monarchy will have to go. The official republicanism of the ARM today is more of a right-wing movement that turns its back on the social democracy so typical of the benign constitutional monarchies, Scandinavia, the Netherlands, Canada and, until now, Australia. Official republicans have no time at all for those who believe that a republic should be about enhancing the opportunities for democratic participation in the government of Australia, many of whom have chosen the name "real republicans". Real republicans, both those in their formal organisation and those outside, are united by a wish to see the popular election of a president of Australia.

As yet there does not seem to be a consensus among real republicans on a precise model. And of course, there is no need to enunciate one for the 1999 referendum. The referendum is only about the Keating–Turnbull republic. At one end of the spectrum real republicans have proposed an almost powerless president on the Irish model – one who would certainly not act as a constitutional referee or umpire, and auditor, as the governor-general does. Power, of course, does not stay in a vacuum, and the power of the referee and auditor would go elsewhere, probably to the prime minister. So most real republicans would attempt to replicate the existing constitution with the president actually being a constitutional umpire. Some would be happy that this could in effect be an antipodean version of the French Fifth Republic, where the powerful executive president and the prime minister "cohabit". A few favour a US-style executive presidency, with a separate legislature. Many of the independent republicans have other agendas. These range across citizen initiative referenda, a bill of rights, greater decentralisation, and other policy areas. Their republicanism is about democracy, and not merely a resort to self-proclaimed patriotism. They see the Keating–Turnbull republic as far worse than the current system, and dangerous.

So what are the main strands of republican sentiment in Australia's history?

THE CONSERVATIVE TRADITION

The nineteenth-century conservative Australian republican was strongly influenced by the American and British republican models. Sir Henry Parkes, the nineteenth-century statesman, was typical. It may seem difficult in the present debate to see the British system as a republic. To Rousseau, Montesquieu, Sir Henry Parkes and, one suspects, most of the nineteenth-century Australian republicans, modern Australia would not only be a republic. It would be an *ideal* republic. Indeed the great leader of Australian Catholics, and Australians of Irish origin, Patrick Cardinal Moran, whose statue stands at the foot of St Mary's Basilica in Sydney, had described the Australian constitutional system as the "most perfect form of republican government". The classical concept of a republic, on which the English model was founded, opposed oppression and tyranny. Above all it feared corruption and patronage. It was not principally a doctrine about monarchy but rather about constitutional rule.

It is not surprising then that the present Australian constitution was influenced by, and embodies, republican principles. Australia goes further even than the famous description of Britain as "a disguised republic". In Australia, the high ceremonial functions of the state, and above all the role of constitutional umpire and auditor are performed by the governor-general and the governors. Sir Henry Parkes himself made this very point in an editorial in *The Empire* in 1853, and members of the Keating–Turnbull school of official republicanism could do well to digest his words:

The word "republic", as everybody ought to know, does not convey any necessary distinction between one form of constitution and another. Every constitution is in reality a republic. There is just as much a republic in England as there is in the United States, the only difference being, that in the one case the word is not used, and in the other it is.

To many federation statesmen, including Henry Parkes, Alfred Deakin, and Ebenezer Syme, a constitution enshrining democratic government would provide all the substantive benefits of republican government – government for the common good. Yet this tradition has gone unobserved in recent years.

Mark McKenna says that Parkes and others, including Australia's first prime minister Edmund Barton, believed that by using the word "commonwealth" a republic had in fact been achieved. He points out that most Australians have yet to appreciate the submerged 'republican' legacy in their present constitution. It is not anti-monarchical or anti-British, but it is a tradition that is inherently suspicious of executive power. It is favourable to checks and balances and the dispersal of power within a federal framework.

The crown then is as much an Australian institution as our English language, our common law, our parliaments. Australian history is after all the history of the development of the colonies under a broad framework for autonomy set by colonial authorities in London and Australia, with the Australian governments operating under and through the crown. Australia may be superficially similar to the United States, but while the very foundation of Australia was a crown initiative, the United States was founded by emigrants wanting to escape the States. The theme of Australian administration is "peace, order and good government". The theme in the United States is famously expressed in the words in the *Declaration of Independence* – "life, liberty and the pursuit of happiness".

There is an important difference between such constitutional monarchies as Australia and Canada, on the one hand, and the United States of America. Ours are social democracies, where development was initiated and led under the crown. We have a tradition of inclusiveness, of the common caring for the under-privileged. The United States is founded on the notion that government should be as minimal as possible to allow the fullest enjoyment of life and liberty and the pursuit of happiness. It is for individuals to succeed by themselves, with minimal or no support from the government.

"PATRIOTIC" REPUBLICANISM

The more radical form of nineteenth-century Australian republicanism is distinguishable from the conservative tradition by its emphasis on nationalism. Dr Mark McKenna argues that this is a Labor tradition. But it was broader than that, and not all those associated with Labor were republicans. Indeed, all Australian Labor prime ministers have been monarchists, with the exception of Bob Hawke and Paul Keating. (Gough Whitlam became a republican after, and probably because of, his dismissal.) The best-known early nationalist republicans came to prominence well before the birth of the Labor Party.

Today, many official republicans seek to frame republicanism as a choice between Australian independence and fealty to the mother country. This was certainly Paul Keating's position, and it was also true of the radical nineteenth-century republicans, at least until the end of the transportation of convicts and the rise of responsible government in Australia.

The great republican figure of the nineteenth-century was undoubtedly the Reverend John Dunmore Lang, a minister of religion. He also had the habit of collecting money from new immigrants on the basis they would immediately receive land grants. They did not. As a result, he was sent to gaol – until his supporters raised sufficient funds to release him. Needless to say, this did not help the reputation of the republican cause. The *Sydney Morning Herald* described Lang as "arrogant, intolerant, and a scheming charlatan".

Parkes and other colonial leaders soon saw that linking republicanism to self-government would be fatal. They distanced themselves from Lang, who attempted to reform his Republican League, with a targeted membership of 10,000. A public meeting was called on Australia Day 1854 for the launch, but only thirty people attended. Lang's bleak republican dawn brings to mind monarchist and politician Tony Abbott's comment that some of the 1993 public meetings across the country called by Paul Keating's Republican Advisory Committee (with generous taxpayer funding and with all those republican celebrities) could have been held in a telephone booth.

While there is a strong nationalistic republican tradition in early Australian history, it seems strange that there is little reference to this by contemporary official republicans who nevertheless loudly appeal to patriotic sentiments. The reason is simple: many of the early nationalist republicans embraced embarrassing doctrines. Late nineteenth-century republicanism was dominated by the *Bulletin*. The *Bulletin*'s republic was to be one which the South African Broederbund would have found very attractive indeed.

In 1888, 40,000 people attended an anti-Chinese demonstration in the Sydney Domain. The *Bulletin* led the movement and said that "Australia had to choose between independence and infection, between the Australian republic and the Chinese leper". The *Bulletin* wanted an Australian form of ethnic cleansing: the expulsion of all Asians. You won't hear much about these racist republican antecedents! Certainly not from Robert Hughes, the Australian-born critic of *Time* magazine, who at a rally in 1996 even tried to demonstrate some tenuous link between those who defend our present constitution and racism.

He overlooked nineteenth-century republicanism.

The *Bulletin* attacked Joseph Chamberlain, colonial secretary, when royal assent was refused to the Queensland *Sugar Works Guarantee Amending Bill*. Why? Because it banned coloured labour!

On 22 June 1901, the year of federation, the *Bulletin* made this hysterical outburst:

If Judas Chamberlain can find a black, or brown or yellow race . . . That has as high a standard of civilisation and intelligence as the whites, that was progressive . . . as brave, as sturdy, as good nation-building material, and that can intermarry with the whites without the mixed progeny showing signs of deterioration, that race is welcome.

So there you have it. The anti-racist crown attacked by the racist republican press!

The *Bulletin*'s racism was to linger well beyond its republicanism. It is only within living memory that it suppressed the motto on its front page masthead: "Australia for the White Man".

It is true that there were attempts by the Labor movement in the 1880s to link the maintenance of monarchical institutions with the persistence of social inequality in Australia. But by the end of the next decade, when Labor politicians began taking their seats in the colonial parliaments – not to mention their oaths of allegiance – it became apparent that reform could best be encouraged through the existing institutions. It was generally agreed that the monarch was no obstacle to reform. The Brisbane *Boomerang*, for instance, explained in 1890 that:

Unless republicanism is thoroughly progressive and democratic practically, as well as nominally, we might as well remain exactly as we are. Because we are discontented with King Log we do not want to place ourselves in the hands of President Stork . . . The republic we want is a land of free men whereon the government rests on the people, and is by them with them and for them. No other form of republicanism will suit us not even though it does a few who follow the will-o-the-wisp of a mere name.

Mark McKenna concludes that the Labor movement realised that Australia's monarchical institutions were as amenable to social democratic government guaranteeing equality as they were to the laissez-faire capitalist policies of the conservatives. It became equally apparent to that most nationalistically republican of journals, the *Bulletin*, that abolition of the monarchy was no longer a practical necessity. It conceded that the monarchy was practically unobjectionable so long as it was understood that the British monarch held his or her position by the will of the nation and for the convenience of the nation. In fact only one delegate at the nineteenth-century conventions argued for the end of the monarchy. And he, George Richard Dibbs, Premier of New South Wales, ended up accepting a knighthood! The *Bulletin* referred to him as Sir George Republican Dibbs and Banjo Paterson wrote in his ballad of G.R. Dibbs:

And he sold the pride of his native land
For a bow and a smile and the shake of the hand.

The realisation that there is little or no reason to complain about a monarchy that is there only as long as the nation wants it, and holds its powers in trust for the nation, has been expressly acknowledged by Queen Elizabeth herself at her golden wedding celebrations at the Guildhall in 1997: ". . . an hereditary constitutional monarchy exists only with the support and consent of the people".

Australia's nineteenth-century nationalist republicanism, while it lasted, was overtly racist and sexist, based on a narrow, isolationist, and exclusive image of Australia as a white man's shed and motivated by fear of Chinese immigration. And these republicans were completely dismissive of Australia's Aboriginal and Torres Strait Islander people. Mark McKenna concludes, "There is no heroic pantheon of republican antecedents in Australia."

A REPUBLIC OF THE ARTS

The arts have had a long association with nationalistic Australian republicanism. It goes back to Henry and Louisa Lawson, who embraced the narrow, racist and isolationist vision of a new Australia espoused by the *Bulletin*. Mark McKenna also includes the painter Adelaide Ironside, and the poet Charles Harpur as "artistic" republicans. In more recent years we have had Donald Horne, Patrick White, Geoffrey Dutton, Les Murray and Arthur Boyd.

McKenna attributes the republicanism of these artists and writers to the strong sense of nationalism they asserted through their work in this seemingly isolated country. Republicanism became a convenient refuge for artists who wished to signify their separation from the "cultural Mecca" of London. They feared a form of psychological dependence that would shackle their creative endeavour in making Australian art.

Concerns about a "cultural cringe" are not new. P.R. Stephensen insisted as long ago as 1936 on the impossibility of a distinctly Australian culture developing while Australia remained intellectually or politically dependent on the British Empire. In the 1960s this sentiment developed significantly, led largely by writers such as Geoffrey Dutton and Donald Horne who spent time in England in the 1960s. But by then, the campaign seemed curiously dated. Weren't these artists fighting yesterday's battles? Hadn't they noticed that the dominant cultural influence in Australia was now that of the United States? As McKenna observes, republicanism was being led by intellectuals who had only belatedly decided that they no longer needed to feel inferior to Britain. Meanwhile most Australians, who identified with Americana, were seeing the revival of Australian film, watching for the first time Australian television dramas, and hearing at least some Australian music. No doubt the average Australian wondered, if they paid any attention at all to the issue, why on earth these intellectuals were worrying about British influence.

So we have the phenomenon of the Australian intelligentsia leading from behind! As French politician Alexandre Auguste

Ledru Rollin exclaimed, "Ah well! I am their leader, I really had to follow them."

Given the profound impact that writer Donald Horne was to have on the later republicans, it is worthwhile to consider more deeply his early approach. The conclusions Horne draws tend to be historical ones, in two senses. From a contemporary perspective they seem to be only of academic interest. His observations about British domination of Australian culture are obviously no longer accurate reflections of Australian society – the Australian sun has long set on British predominance. But his conclusions are also historical in that he spends a great deal of time discussing the problem of past perceptions of Australia, rather than those which prevail today.

He wrote that for the extreme empire loyalists of the past, loyalty was primarily a matter of the empire and the monarch. Loyalty was due to Australia precisely because Australia *was* "British". To the extent that Australians deviated from "Britishness" they denied their heritage and their destiny. Even to distinguish between the interests of Australia and Britain was disloyal.

It is telling that even in 1965 Horne preferred to address the problematic mentality that existed in Australia in the past tense.

His pre-1975 republican views are also interesting in the extent to which they depart from present arguments. In 1965 Horne argued that the maintenance of Australia as a monarchy did immense harm. It delayed the final awakening for the generations that still ran the country. It confused and disgusted the younger generation. He went so far as to say that the perpetuation of this "burdensome fiction" made us a "nothing" country wallowing in "inadequacy and despair". And, anticipating the many arguments that republicans would later use, he predicted an immense sense of creative release would come when Australia elected its first president.

Donald Horne would probably be depressed by a series of opinion polls in the nineties which show that the youth of the country, like their grandparents, are less republican then their parents. The "Absolutely Fabulous" effect.

Forgetting the example of Canada, Horne claimed the crisis was that Australia has no identity and its only hope is to pursue republicanism. So the republic is necessary because Australia lacks an identity. This is a view that poet Les Murray has also enunciated. At a republican rally in 1977 he said that the prospect of living one's whole life in a timid, late-colonial society was galling. If the republic is about anything, he insisted, it is about the dignity and potential of human beings in this country. It is about "rejecting slurs", "casting off the psychological impediments to action", "confirming and strengthening the confidence of every Australian". Yet polling shows consistently that Australians are not at all interested in the question of the republic. And most foreigners who know Australians would be equally surprised.

Les Murray's views are in stark contrast to sentiments expressed by merchant banker and ARM leader Malcolm Turnbull in his opening address to the Constitutional Convention in February 1998. Turnbull reflected on his perception of Australia during the Bicentennial celebrations. He said there was nothing wrong with our nation. Australia became a proud and independent country years ago. He claimed that a republic would affirm a nation not defined by race, religion, colour or cultural background. Our nationhood, he said, is defined by our commitment to each other and our commitment to those uniquely Australian political values of freedom, tolerance and a fair go. So, for him, a republic would be merely an affirmation of what we are.

Turnbull would seem to be on even thinner ice than Horne. Horne proclaimed the urgent need to found a new identity. Turnbull's republic would merely affirm what we are. So why do we need it?

A SECOND WIND

The dismissal of the Whitlam government in 1975 changed the republican debate. What was a curious academic school, the obsession with a cultural cringe, suddenly had legs. It is worth recalling the immediate causes of the 1975 crisis. They were Leader of the Opposition Malcolm Fraser's impatience for government and the

Whitlam government's indication that it would try to govern without supply, that is without the authorisation of funding by parliament. It was the governor-general's decision to act before supply ran out that brought the crisis to an end. The crisis was in no way caused, provoked or exacerbated by the queen. But logic is not necessarily a guide for political action, and many blamed the monarchy, rather than the politicians who had actually caused the crisis.

So the dismissal provided a new source of republican sentiment. Until then the Labor Party had been as monarchist as the Liberal and Country Parties. Leaders such as John Curtin, Dr Evatt and Ben Chifley were as royalist in sentiment and in action as R.G. Menzies. After all, it was our great wartime prime minister, John Curtin, who recommended that a Royal Duke be governor-general!

But in July 1981, six years after Whitlam's dismissal, a national conference of the Labor Party voted to support a republic. There were in fact two motions, this one from the floor, and another from the executive, asking for an inquiry on the subject and a report. According to the historian Alan Atkinson, the motion from the executive should have been put first, but Neville Wran, the national president, gave priority to the motion from the floor. It was carried unanimously. Labor was committed to a republic without any form of consultation or discussion within the broader party. A motion in 1991 for a public education campaign, culminating in a referendum to make Australia an "independent" republic on 1 January 2001 was carried – but "not very vigorously", according to the then ALP president.

What then are we to make of something being official ALP policy? The first platform of the ALP aimed for the total exclusion of "coloured and other undesirable races".

For many years Labor was committed to the widespread nationalisation of industry and the banks. Both of these policies have not only been abandoned, but reversed. Will republicanism stay as ALP official policy? Whatever the policy, polling in 1999 indicated that at least 40 per cent of Labor voters intended to vote No in the 1999 referendum.

Before he endured the indignity of dismissal, Gough Whitlam was asked whether it was correct that he wished to transform the governor-generalship into a presidency. He replied:

No, I do not think that is said. I have used the term that the governor-general is viceroy and some people seem to think that is an extraordinary concept but constitutionally it is quite obvious. He is the stand-in for the Queen when she is not in residence here. He can do everything that she can do as head of state. The system of governor-general works quite well. After all, no government of any political complexion can be better pleased than with a system where the head of state, the ceremonial head, holds the position for a certain number of years on the nomination of the national head of government. The system works very well and our governors-general, certainly the Australian ones, have always been top men.

So before his dismissal Mr Whitlam clearly thought the Australian system quite agreeable. He is of course entitled to change his views. In 1983 he wrote that he believed not merely in a symbolic change, but in large-scale substantive alterations to the constitution. The case for a republic, he says, is not primarily directed against the monarchy "but against the faults" in the Australian constitution. He believes that the case rests not so much on the need to sever links with the crown, but on the need to strengthen Australia's own institutions and democratic safe-guards. He says any worthwhile improvement of the constitution will require major changes, and "since the monarchy is integral to, and virtually inseparable from, the constitution as it stands, the only realistic course is to replace it altogether". (Arnold, 258)

The action of Sir John Kerr certainly gave a renewed impetus to the cause of republicanism in Australia. A former governor-general, Sir Zelman Cowan, points out that a republic, of itself, would not necessarily dispose of the problem of the exercise of such discretions. But the fact that a governor-general, "unelected and the representative of the queen", acted in this way is seen by some – perhaps by a growing number of Australians – as grounds for remaking the constitution without monarchical institutions and representation. He believes the achievement of "full" independence for Australia, the changing pattern of her relationships in the world, and the changing character and composition of Australian society and the Australian people have all affected our view of the special relationship with Britain and its institutions. (Arnold, 287–88)

Mark McKenna says that the modern push for a republic had its roots in Donald Horne's response to the dismissal. Horne saw a need to remove the monarchy not only to assert our national identity, but also to democratise the constitution. McKenna points out that Australians are reluctant to endorse constitutional change. So Horne's republic might sink quickly if it were too closely linked with substantive changes to the constitution. (McKenna, 236)

Isolating the republic as a mere question of patriotism, of national identity, from the problem of substantive reform is precisely the approach embodied in the ARM's platform. This has the added advantage of avoiding what Australians have traditionally done in referenda – looking closely at the details of the proposed change.

SUNDAY LUNCH IN WOOLLAHRA: THE AUSTRALIAN REPUBLICAN MOVEMENT IS ESTABLISHED

The smouldering passion for revenge ignited by the 1975 dismissal was directed at the crown, and only relatively briefly at Malcolm Fraser. Yet Fraser had forced the issue and taken the country to the brink. Ironically now a republican, he has escaped the ignominy that was directed at Sir John Kerr. Little blame today is attached to Gough Whitlam who, through his wit, fine sense of humour and patrician elegance, today enjoys a high standing in Australian life. But his new found republican mission would have been dissipated had it not been given form in the creation of the Australian Republican Movement and had it not become part of Prime Minister Paul Keating's "big picture".

The Australian Republican Movement was not born in such

heroic circumstances as were the *Declaration of Independence*, the *Magna Carta* or the *Declaration of the Rights of Man*. Rather, according to republican writer Thomas Keneally, it came about over lunch with Malcolm Turnbull, in the exclusive Sydney suburb of Woollahra:

That lunch at Jill Hickson's and Neville Wran's table had now reached the point where nearly all the fish they bought the day before at the Sydney Fish Markets had been eaten. In a manner all too typical of generous Sunday lunches in Sydney, a number of bottles of Hunter Valley Chardonnay had also been drained. Neville Wran leaned over the table and said, "The other thing I want to see happen before I bloody well die is an Australian republic." (Keneally, 77)

McKenna says that Keneally's description of a "boozy lunch", while honest, was not particularly astute: wine as the wellspring of the Australian republic! The concept of a group of citizens leading the republican debate proved to be effective, but it would also lend itself to allegations of elitism. The ARM, McKenna says, was not so much a people's movement as a "media-offensive by a minority of influential individuals who claimed to have the people's interest at heart".

The argument that the ARM's approach is elitist has also been expressed by other republicans. In 1995, launching Tony Abbott's book *The Minimal Monarchy*, long-time republican Les Murray declared that in some circles, "I am probably a notorious old republican ... Have I turned away from all that suddenly and become a royalist?" No! He said that, on the contrary, "I've become more of a republican lately, out of fear of the ugly, elite republic towards which we are being rushed at the moment – the republic of celebrities and hectoring and social scorn." Murray said that Australians glibly assume there is such a thing as freedom of speech – but for most people there is not. People are going to be punished with extreme social opprobrium if they express certain opinions which are not on the agenda. They can lose their social life, their sexual life, and their jobs. He remembered an

Australia where people knew how to differ and how to soothe difference into civility. Since the 1960s, Australian thought and debate had been controlled by a group who had solidified into "a para-government of boards and quangos" beyond the reach of elected ministers. This para-government, in concert with a complacent media, has tyrannised society with "unpopular, un-voted-for social change" ever since. He said that he would not dare vote for a republic while those 1960s ideas were stuck in the heads of most of his generation who belong to the elite, stifling them, intoxicating them and blinding them to their own country and people. I think we need a respite until the temper of our society changes. Tony's absentee monarchy may have to do until then. I can't think of anything better . . . What's best for Australia . . . [is] the only question worth asking in this constitutional debate. (*Australian*, 3 October 1995, p 1–2)

An anonymous internal report leaked to the press expressed similar concerns about the ARM's leadership. Later in the same month, the *Australian* reported that the ARM had come under attack from within its own ranks for being controlled by a "Sydney dinner party set" and being anti-democratic.

A document prepared within one of the movement's state branches also claimed many potential members resent the "brash, egocentric, sometimes overbearing, sometimes bullying personal style" of its chairman, Malcolm Turnbull. More recently a fundraising function in Melbourne was described as one where the champagne was decent and the canapes okay, but the timing and placement were terribly wrong. "It was a night to forget. Mostly because so many republicans cannot bear to remember it without wincing." (Virginia Trioli, *Bulletin*, 30 March 1999) With photographs of the opulent evening splashed across the daily press, the *Bulletin* said the event produced the answer to only one question of any importance: where do osprey feathers actually come from? Answer, they come from society leader, Susan Renouf!

A NEW PRIME MINISTER WITH VISIONS

The ALP platform, disgruntled artists and the Australian Republican Movement – even together – were not enough to make republicanism a *real* political force. Everything was to change when Paul Keating overthrew Bob Hawke in the Labor caucus.

Keating's prime ministership was based on his (big picture) image as a leader seeking national re-invigoration and new definitions of Australian identity. He was never without an opportunity to speak on these issues: even when announcing the Australian of the Year in 1995, Keating managed to reduce Arthur Boyd's entire artistic *oeuvre* to an attempt to distil the essence of Australia on canvas!

As Alan Atkinson says, politicians – especially Keating – are often confused about what they mean by Australian identity. Sometimes they mean our profile in the world; sometimes what they think about themselves. "If he feels more excited and distinctive as a leader among leaders, it ought to follow (in his view) that we should feel more significant as Australians." It is the prime minister's task, Atkinson says, to build our profile in the world. It is not Australians' task to colour themselves to match his profile.

For a government that had been almost a decade in power and was about to go to the polls at a time of high unemployment and economic recession, the republic provided Keating with a means of reinvigorating the government and distinguishing his prime ministership from that of his predecessor. He used it, too, to paint the Liberals as un-Australian and to distract Labor supporters from his free market policies.

Keating's drive for a republic was encouraged by Paul Kelly, then editor-in-chief of Rupert Murdoch's *Australian* newspaper. From the time of Keating's appointment as prime minister, the *Australian* maintained a consistently pro-republican line, regularly leading editorials with sympathetic headlines such as "Our republic a historical opportunity".

The trail set by the *Australian* was to be followed even more vigorously in more recent years by the *Sydney Morning Herald*. Once Sydney's conservative newspaper, the *Herald*, relieved of the patrician stewardship of the Fairfax family, has given itself over to a series of small 'l' liberal causes. Newspaper editors around the country have followed. Now, an editor or journalist who is not a republican is a rare bird indeed.

Soon, a number of Liberal politicians were to come out as republicans.

This sudden rush of republicanism among the political establishment and the elites is remarkable, given that only eight years ago the mere suggestion that republicanism would play a central role in Australian politics would have been thought absurd. The fortuitous convergence of a Labor prime minister wearing a streak of republican nationalism like a badge of honour, the London media's intrusion into private lives of the Royal Family and the birth of the ARM, have assisted the growth of republicanism. But this was still essentially a *vague* idea of republicanism, not a specific model.

For the ARM, Keating and the *Australian*, there has been a common desire to address what they see as a need for a singularly Australian concept of national identity that would not be shared with Britain, nor presumably with Canada or even New Zealand. There is still no indication that broader issues will be addressed by republicanism. And the evidence is that Australians generally are not interested in going down this path. In February 1999 the *Bulletin* Morgan Poll on the three most important things the "federal government should be doing something about" ranked "the republic vs the monarchy and flag issues" at 4 per cent, up from 1 per cent. Employment (53 per cent), health (37 per cent) and education (35 per cent) were the leading issues. And this was after years of massive media promotion of republican issues, as well as the government created and funded Republic Advisory Committee and the Constitutional Convention of 1998.

Historians and political scientists have discussed narrow republicanism for years. But this discussion has remained limited to the elite, found mainly in academia and the opinion pages of the broadsheet press. While the rhetoric is about a republic as a vehicle for 'inclusion', there are few signs that Australian women or Australian Aboriginals are about to lead the republican charge. That official, ARM, Keating–Turnbull republicanism has little or nothing to do with Australian identity is illustrated by a curious incident in 1993. The ARM, with enormous public relations and media resources, announced a surprise recruit to an incredulous public. This was none other than a once well-loved Australian cartoon character, the koala Blinky Bill. There was, as Alan Atkinson notes, a rich symbolism in this. The new Blinky Bill had big smooth ears, a smaller nose, and more globular cheeks than "any healthy koala" should have. His eyes were "Walt Disney rather than Dorothy Wall". He wore his trousers in the US style – one strap across the shoulder. This was a Disney character with the words "Blinky Bill" on him. But it was really Mickey Mouse. How appropriate for a republican movement whose leaders espouse all of the doctrines of globalisation.

The republican debate in Australia has narrowed to a point where the agitators now concede that the aims of the official republicanism are actually embraced by the existing constitution. The Republic Advisory Committee even admitted that it may be appropriate to regard Australia as a "crowned republic".

There has also been a partial concession made in the nationalist republican debate now that the "cultural cringe" has absolutely no relevance. The republic is now claimed to be only about how to express the Australian identity. It is no longer whether the Australian identity is distinct from a British one. Everybody knows that it is, and probably always was. As Mark McKenna writes, the republican debate is therefore no longer about whether we are British or Australian – it is about "how we wish to be Australian".

Official ARM republicans would do well to remember the wisdom that prevailed a century ago when our present constitution was adopted. Henry Parkes said that our constitutional system would "not come to meet with wild ravings of some person who may call out 'Republicanism', without the slightest knowledge of what he is talking about". (*Constitution Papers*, 92)

2
THE CASE FOR A REPUBLIC

In 1999 Australians will at last be allowed to vote on what ARM spokesman Thomas Keneally correctly describes as the biggest structural change to the constitution since Federation (Channel Nine, *Nightline*, January 1998). It must be stressed that they are not going to vote on "*a* republic". That would be so imprecise as to be meaningless. They will vote on a specific republican model, the best model that the ARM, the official republicans, have been able to develop over the best part of the decade.

While there would have been no political difficulty in putting a referendum to the Australian people during the years 1993 to 1996 when Mr Keating was prime minister, the people were never given an opportunity to vote on the first republican model. Yet we saw Mr Keating frequently telling world leaders about his policy to turn Australia into a republic: German Chancellor Kohl (while apparently also advising him how to redesign Berlin), French President Mitterand, and former Indonesian President Suharto. It is reported that when M. Mitterand heard this exciting news, he took Keating into the room of the Elysee Palace kept just as Napoleon had left it – a room dedicated to *delusions de grandeur*. One mischievous journalist had already dubbed the prime minister the "Bonaparte from Bankstown".

While ARM spokesmen regularly proclaim their patriotism, it is curious that they so often worry what the neighbours think. Of course, if the truth be known, our neighbours on the whole are not much concerned about our constitution, apart from applauding our stability as a democracy. As Lee Kuan Yew, the Singaporean statesman, said: "I don't think Asia understands what the argument is about. Australia would not generate greater esteem in Asia as a republic . . ." (*Australian Financial Review*, 19 April 1994).

This republican cultural cringe recalls the curious practice of journalists asking international celebrities just as they come off planes at Sydney's Kingsford Smith airport: "What do you think of Australia?" To which actress Vivien Leigh is said to have replied, "If you'd get out of the way, I'd be able to see it."

Does it matter that Australia, and particularly its parliament and its media, have been so distracted by this debate over the best part of a decade? Well, there have been both transparent and hidden costs for the country.

The transparent cost, from the point of the taxpayer, can be calculated. It would include the costs of the Republic Advisory Committee, the Constitutional Convention and the referendum: in the order of $120 million. There are other public costs in changes made even before the referendum by way of surreptitious replacement of symbols all over the country, in town halls, government offices, stationery and so on.

Then there is the hidden cost of the distraction. The simple wages costs in terms of the time spent by government ministers, parliamentarians and public servants must be considerable. And what about the "opportunity costs"? Time spent worrying about a republic could have been devoted to the economy, trade, education, unemployment, health, or law and order.

That is why the debate has to stop somewhere, and why the referendum is overdue. Among the many arguments put for Australia becoming a republic, you will never hear that the change will save money. The contribution made by the Australian taxpayer for the upkeep of the royal palaces, the court, the monarch and the Royal Family is . . . nothing. Not a cent. And it is as sure as night follows day that when the president, the deputy presidents and the state governors take office that the costs of their accommodation, offices, staff, travel arrangements and, retirement benefits will be substantially increased to mirror their greater importance.

Then will come the costs to the changes to stationery, insignia, flags, uniforms, postage stamps, and the currency. Some claim that cost will go into billions apart, of course, from the costs of a constitution if it does not function properly when it is most needed.

Many reasons for change have been suggested. They range from the pathetic, to the ludicrous, to the superficially plausible.

DIPLOMACY

One of the most unusual reasons is that advanced by some former diplomats who constantly refer to the difficulty they have in explaining our "confusing" constitution to, for example, the former Indonesian dictator. Apparently President Suharto could not understand why Mr Whitlam, a democrat, actually accepted the fact that Sir John Kerr dismissed him. Presumably a dictator would have reacted differently. In such situations presidents usually claim to be acting for the people. The reader can imagine the scene in the presidential palace. President Suharto is seated at a desk, and the Australian Ambassador is giving the latest in an interminable series of lectures on such exciting subjects as section 92 of the Australian constitution. They have reached the topic on the governor-general, and the Ambassador has recounted how and why Mr Whitlam's commission was withdrawn and that Mr Whitlam, unable or not interested in contacting the queen, went to the Lodge and had lunch. The general interrupts, saying, "But why didn't he just arrest the governor-general?" Perhaps some of our diplomats should concentrate more on their core activities rather than acting as advisers on the Australian constitution.

THE REPUBLIC WILL STOP THE BRAIN DRAIN, ARTHRITIS ETC

Sir David Smith has assembled the more bizarre reasons advanced for a republic in a paper to the Samuel Griffiths Society in 1998. Among those he listed are:

- Al Grassby, a minister of the crown in the Whitlam Labor government, told us that the monarchy was responsible for the recession of the late 1980s, for the one million Australians who were unemployed for the business excesses of that period, and for the exodus from Australia of our top scientists. (*Canberra Times*, 8 December 1993)

- Michael Lynch, general manager of the Australia Council for the Arts and the Opera House 1998, said that the monarchy stifles artistic talent and prevents our artists from fully expressing themselves. (*Australian*, 25 October 1994)

- Sir Anthony Mason, former high court judge, confessed that he started to become a republican at the age of eight, while watching a cricket Test match between Australia and England during the 1932/33 bodyline series. Sir David observes "it would seem that he waited for sixty-five years before revealing it". (*Australian*, 28 October 1997)

- Janet Holmes à Court, an Australian Republican Movement representative, told a delegation from the British Chamber of Commerce that she wanted a new flag and a new constitution because an Asian cabinet minister had told her that his country would help the Australian people in their struggle for independence from Britain. It also worries her that her Asian acquaintances are confused by the queen's portrait hanging on Australian Embassy walls. (*Canberra Times*, 26 March 1998, *Age*, 7 November 1997) It was later reported that "given her head, Janet Holmes à Court's republic would experiment with radical drug cures and legalise many illicit substances, possibly even heroin": *Australian*, 6 November 1997. Later she was to explain that her republicanism was not anti-British. Did she not, she said, employ hundreds of Britons in her UK operations?

- Sallyanne Atkinson, former Lord Mayor of Brisbane, former Australian Trade Commissioner to France, and an ARM delegate, said that she was republican because she found the French "confused" by the fact that the Queen of England was also Queen of Australia. (*Australian*, 8 October 1997). Sir

David Smith comments that he should have thought that surely the French have been more confused by the fact that, following their bloody revolution of 1789 and the execution of their monarchy, they endured the Reign of Terror, Empire under Emperor Napoleon, restoration of the Monarchy, the second French Empire, Republics One, Two, Three and Four, and the Vichy government that collaborated with the Nazis during World War II, before President de Gaulle gave them their current Fifth Republic. The Trade Commissioner, he says, might more usefully have spent her time in Paris in telling the French something of the enduring stability of our constitutional arrangements.

- Bill Ferris, former Chairman of the Board of the Australian Trade Commission and now the Chairman of the Australian Venture Capital Association, told us that the republic would present a windfall marketing opportunity for Australian exporters because our present constitutional arrangements were harmful to the overseas promotion of our products and services. According to Mr Ferris, the republic will help us gain international recognition for our technology and our inventions, and will ensure that much more venture capital than at present will flow back into our newer industries (*Australian*, 10 October 1997). Sir David comments: "So now we know – the monarchy is responsible for our trade deficit!" (Mr Ferris more recently argued that the change was essential to promoting investment in local corporations. (*Sydney Morning Herald* 16/10/98)

- Lindsay Fox, founder and chairman of Fox Group Holdings and an Australian Republican Movement delegate, together with other business leaders, saw the republic as an opportunity for Australia to "re-badge" and "re-band" itself, thus reducing the nation, its history, its constitution and its system of government to the level of a new car or a packet of detergent. (*Business Review Weekly*, 10 November 1997, *Australian Financial Review*, 24 January 1998)

- Neville Wran, former premier of New South Wales and an

Australian Republican Movement delegate, told us that changing to a republic would boost jobs and invigorate Australia's spirits (*Australian Financial Review*, 20 November 1997)

There are other examples. Former Deputy Lord Mayor of Sydney Henry Tsang claimed: "People in Asia are confused. They want to invest here or start a new business in Australia but they are puzzled." He finds it embarrassing explaining to Asian business people "why Australia clings to the Queen" when "England is a small nation on its way down ..." (*City of Sydney Times*, 27 January 1999)

Simone Young, conductor of the Australian Opera and Ballet Orchestra said: "I feel very strongly about it because I'm identified as belonging to the English cultural scene and I'm very, very adamantly Australian." She said many "ex-pat" Australian artists who have settled in the UK are often mistakenly thought of in other countries as being British. But Canadians in the US or in France have similar problems. The solution perhaps relates to changing their accent and their address. Or just not worrying about such an insignificant matter. (*Australian*, 15 March 1999)

What will be next? "Republicanism, the miracle cure for arthritis"?

THE BRITISH INHERITANCE

Former diplomat, Richard Woolcott, seems to have spent many hours with foreigners trying unsuccessfully to explain our "confusing" constitution. He is terribly worried about the fact that the Queen of Australia is also the Queen of Canada, and especially the Queen of the United Kingdom. He says a Spaniard observed that no similar connection with the Spanish royal family would be possible in any former Spanish colony. (*Sydney Morning Herald*, 9 January 1998)

You only need to read a little of the history of the two empires to understand why. For example, compare Australia today with the most promising of the former Spanish colonies at the time of federation, Argentina, to understand the differences between the British and Spanish empires.

It is the British inheritance that has made Australia so consistently a rich, open, democratic and generous society. As a consequence, she chose to fight tyranny in two world wars. This was unlike the former Spanish colonies, who mostly remained neutral, at least until an Allied victory was inevitable. It is worth spending a few moments to try to understand what the British inheritance means to Australia, and why it cannot be compared to the Spanish bequest to Latin America, which in cultural terms should not be underestimated. The point is that the positive British contribution to Australia is not only cultural in the narrow sense, it is economic, political and social. Spain contributed little in democratic stable government for her colonies. She could not, for democracy was unknown at home.

David Landes argues that Britain gave people elbow room. Political and civil freedoms won first for the nobles were extended by war, usage, and law to the common folk. To all of these gains one can oppose exceptions: Britain had its poor, and knew abuses of privilege, distinctions of class and status, concentrations of wealth and power, marks of preference and favour. But everything is relative, and by the seventeenth century at least in comparison to most other countries, the British were free and fortunate.

Britain was, Landes says, a precociously modern, industrial nation, with the salient ability of a successful society to transform itself to adapt to new things and ways. One key area of change was the increasing freedom and security of the people. Nothing, he says, did more for enterprise. Yet until recently the British called themselves *subjects* of the crown, although Landes says they have for longer than anywhere else been *citizens*.

That freedom continued to develop in Britain and was taken to the colonies. The American colonies were the most liberated in the world. And the lesson of their War of Independence was not lost on the British. They learned that the colonies would want to tax and to govern themselves.

Australia remained in the Empire in 1901 because it wanted to. Richard Woolcott suggests that to a Spaniard the prospect of a personal union between the Spanish crown and, say, an

Argentinian crown is impossible. From this he draws the conclusion that the personal union between the British, Australian, Canadian, New Zealand and other crowns must be forthwith dissolved. As Mr Woolcott must know, there is no analogy.

I WON'T BECOME AN AUSTRALIAN!

Perhaps the most surprising argument for a republic is that advanced by foreigners who choose to live in Australia but who insist that we must change our constitution before they will graciously accept citizenship.

A few years ago the *Australian* ran a cartoon showing a cranky looking immigrant coming down a gangplank onto a quay where the Australian flag was flying. An eager Australian says, "Welcome to Australia, mate. Is there anything we can do?" The immigrant snarls, "The first thing you can do is change that bloody flag." Fortunately few immigrants take such an attitude.

But we have seen the isolated case where a foreign resident, invariably a member of the "chattering class", sets out the conditions for taking Australia nationality. I can recall two university teachers telling me they could not become Australians while Elizabeth was our queen. One, an Irish woman, admitted somewhat sheepishly that she already also had a British passport – and therefore presumably owed allegiance to the Queen of the United Kingdom.

Perhaps the most remarkable position was that adopted in 1998 by Paul McGeough, Irish citizen and editor of the *Sydney Morning Herald*. "As soon as this country stands on its own two feet with its own head of state and becomes a real country, then I'll be a citizen of it." (*Daily Telegraph*, 10 October 1998)

To the views of immigrants we can add those of expatriates returning, and even, of visitors. Sinn Fein leader Mr Gerry Adams, while visiting Australia, urged Australians to vote "Yes" in the coming referendum. Why? "I don't have time for monarchies of any kind. For my entire life I have been involved in opposition to British interference in my affairs." He then proceeded to instruct Australia on its responsibilities in East Timor. (*Sun Herald*,

28 February 1999) If Mr Adams objects to what he sees as British interference in his country's affairs, why does he think it appropriate for him to interfere in Australia's?

UNLIKELY PREDICTIONS

There is nothing new in the making of unlikely predictions about the benefits that will flow from a republic or from some major political change. New Zealanders not long ago were persuaded to change their voting system to one which would be more democratic. Their MMP system was said by many to mean "Many More Politicians".

After the first election it took about three months to form a government. This was led by the same prime minister New Zealanders thought they were voting out in coalition with the New Zealand First Party, which had assured voters that a vote for them was a vote against the party which became their coalition partners. And who led the push for change? Yes, the now retired editor of a leading New Zealand newspaper.

Nobody yet is on record as saying a republic will ensure that we are never again at war, but at the end of the eighteenth-century philosopher Immanuel Kant believed that wars would diminish as monarchies became republics. A vain hope. He was not to know of the French and Russian revolutions, nor of Hitler's republic. But at least Kant did not exclude constitutional monarchies from his republican prescription.

"IT'S YOUR LAST CHANCE!" OR "WORSE WILL COME!"

Salesman often use this argument to persuade a potential buyer to "close the deal". It is hardly appropriate in a constitutional debate, but it is used by the ARM when it claims that this may be the last chance to vote for a republic. There is, of course, no reason why a second or even third referendum could not be proposed. Some topics have been put to the Australian people five times!

Alternatively, Australians are warned that they had better vote for this model, otherwise worse will come. Professor Greg Craven, a nominated delegate to the convention argues this.

Although once a monarchist, then a neo-monarchist and then a critic of the model to be voted on, he fears that if it is rejected, another model based on the direct election of the president will be proposed. He assumes that the government of the day will put up a model which is unworkable, and that the people will actually vote for it. This demonstrates little confidence in the Australian people. A people who on their record have demonstrated considerable wisdom in these matters.

KEATING ATTACKS THE CONSTITUTION

As we have seen, it was Paul Keating who made changing Australia into a republic a major political objective. But he knew that he would have to have a good argument to make the vast changes to our constitution necessary to effect this.

An old approach has been to describe ours as a "horse and buggy" constitution. No American says that of theirs – and it is more than twice as old. Although it tolerated slavery, and did not forestall the civil war, it is still revered by Americans. But Keating went further, suggesting our constitution was forced on an unwilling people. On more than one occasion Keating claimed the constitution was drafted and imposed by the British Foreign Office. His listeners' immediate reaction must have been that surely he meant the Colonial Office. In any event the prime minister was soon reminded that our constitution was in fact drafted in Australia, by Australians. And unlike the United States or Canada, our constitution was actually approved by the Australian people in each of the States, not just by the politicians.

AN AUSTRALIAN HEAD OF STATE

So Mr Keating fell silent, briefly. Then he changed tack. The republic was, he now claimed, only about having an Australian as head of state. (In fact we first had one almost seventy years ago, with the appointment of Sir Isaac Isaacs in 1930.)

The difficulty was that at first few Australians understood what he was talking about. And since then few Australians have cared. In the English-speaking world the term "head of state" is normally only used by diplomats, international lawyers, and other worthies. And, of course, now the ARM.

Having sought to impose on the Australian consciousness this arcane concept of head of state, the ARM resorts to three other associated arguments, all deceptions or inventions. First, they deny that the crown is an Australian institution. Second, they claim that the queen is a foreign citizen. Third, they argue that we have no say in the succession.

THE AUSTRALIAN CROWN

The *Balfour Declaration*, 1926, recognised something that had already evolved. Australia, and the other dominions were now "equal in status, in no way subordinate one to another in any aspect of their domestic or external affairs, though united by a common allegiance to the crown, and freely associated, as members of the British Commonwealth of Nations". This was given statutory effect by the *Statute of Westminster*, 1931, so that the former single indivisible crown of an empire had become several crowns of a commonwealth of independent nations.

When the Australian parliament last dealt with this issue in 1973, it agreed that "the royal style and titles appertaining to the crown" were not in accord with "current constitutional relationships within the British commonwealth". The parliament then changed the queen's title by deleting reference to the United Kingdom but retaining the existing title "Queen of Australia", which had been adopted in 1953. The office, as a separate office, probably existed in 1926 and certainly existed by 1931.

In the case of *Sue v Hill* (23 June 1999), the high court decided that Mrs Hill could not take her place as a senator, because, in breach of the constitution, she owed allegiance to Britain, a foreign power. In fact she was a dual citizen. The court affirmed that Australia was independent and that the Australian crown is by law and convention a separate institution from the British crown – or the Canadian, or New Zealand crown.

In doing so the crown has become adapted to Australian conditions. It is as Australian as our beaches and our forests. The same has happened to that other import, the parliament. The British legal system has also become Australian, and so has our use of the language we share with Canada, New Zealand and other countries.

To demonstrate our independence, need we throw out our Australian legal system because it is a British import? Should we throw out our Australian parliaments, our Australian English language, merely because they originally came from Britain? The answer must surely be No. So why should we reject that other indigenous institution, the crown – our independent, non-political constitutional referee and auditor – merely because it comes from Britain?

One of Australia's most distinguished international lawyers, Professor D.P. O'Connell, who was to hold the chair of international law at Oxford, refers to the historical fact that the "personal union" of several crowns, one person occupying two or more thrones, is well-known and well-established in history and in law. So the Queen of Australia is a separate institution, but the same person as the Queen of Canada fills that office.

THE FOREIGN QUEEN

The second deception is the often-repeated claim that the queen is a foreign citizen. She is in fact neither foreign nor a citizen. The queen is not a citizen of Canada. Nor is she a foreigner in Canada. She is *Queen* of Canada. As she is *Queen* of New Zealand. The queen is not even a citizen of the United Kingdom, nor a foreigner there. She is the *Queen* of the United Kingdom. And the same goes for Australia.

The law is quite clear. To say she is a foreigner, to call her the "foreign queen" is incorrect. Merely because she lives overseas does not make her foreign. Otherwise many Australians, including many distinguished ones like Robert Hughes, would not be Australians.

It is strange that the argument about a foreign queen is used, when foreign influences are so strong in Australia. They have even intruded into the debate about our flag.

In 1997, when the *Sydney Morning Herald* and Ausflag began a competition for a new flag, two foreign multinationals became sponsors!

International bodies, usually part of the United Nations or associated organisations have played an intrusive role in internal Australian matters in recent years. Whether it is our environmental standards, human rights, Aboriginal affairs, or, most recently, mining legislation, we have found such bodies increasingly interfering in our affairs. That the members of these committees are often from countries with lower standards in environmental protection, racial discrimination or democratic practice is ironic. Yet many who call for a republic, who paint the queen as foreign, approve of increasing involvement in Australian affairs by international bureaucracies often closely associated with authoritarian governments.

And those who would paint the queen as foreign are often the proponents of globalisation, the removal of power from the democratic nation state to unregulated international economic forces. The pinnacle of these are the unregulated markets that have turned money, once a means of exchange and a store of value, into a tradeable commodity. The international "invisible hand" is supposed to provide us with continuity and improve progress.

The exercise of foreign economic power within the nation state is not always seen as a good thing. Goldman Sach's, the US bank, apologised to the Thai government in 1999 for a letter the government saw as damaging the economy. In the same year a leading Japanese merchant bank was found to have traded in breach of Australian law.

The point for our purposes is not whether foreign economic power is good or bad. The point is that foreign influence in Australia has not previously been as strong as it is today.

And the strongest supporters of this foreign influence are frequently to be found in republican ranks.

THE SUCCESSION

The third deception is that we have no say in the succession. Again this is wrong. After all, it was Australian prime minister Joe Lyons who stressed to the British prime minister that the proposed marriage of Edward VII to Wallis Simpson was unacceptable.

The preamble to the *Statute of Westminster* of 1931 states clearly that: "any alteration in the law relating to the succession to the Throne ... shall hereafter require the assent of all the Parliaments". And this includes the Australian parliament.

So if there are aspects concerning the succession which do not seem appropriate today, it is a matter obviously for discussion between governments, then for legislation by the relevant parliaments.

There are many arguments for a republic. We are about to come to the preferred argument of the ARM, an Australian head of state.

There are just as many responses which can be put to those arguments.

The essential point is that the referendum is not about "*the*" republic, or whether Australians would prefer a republic. It is whether the model on offer is better than – or at least as good as – our existing constitution.

3
THE HEAD OF STATE

The real question in the coming referendum is whether Australians approve of a change to a republic in which the president is chosen by a two-thirds majority vote of a joint sitting in parliament, but where he holds office at the whim of the prime minister. The latter point will not actually appear in the question. But as it will be unique in the world, it ought to be there.

The Australian Republican Movement is attempting to portray the question as: "Do you want an Australian as head of state?" This is in fact the very question Paul Keating proposed putting to the people in a plebiscite, which would have had no legal effect. The plebiscite did not proceed when it was first proposed because ACM indicated supporters would be advised to vote Yes, as we already have an Australian as head of state. Nevertheless, considerable public and private resources have been put into promoting the message that we need an Australian head of state. It was the core theme of the report of the Republic Advisory Committee and the core of the ARM's television advertising campaign for the Constitutional Convention. (That this was the *only* TV advertising campaign is testimony to the vast financial resources available to the ARM.) No doubt it will be at the heart of a taxpayer-funded Yes campaign in October. That the ARM tried to substitute a question similar to this for the question in the referendum is testimony to Paul Keating's continuing influence in the republican debate.

This argument is spurious. It is used to avoid debating the actual question that is being asked in the referendum. The question is: "Do you approve of the proposed law to establish the Commonwealth of Australia as a republic with the queen and governor-general being replaced by a president appointed by a two-thirds majority of the members of the commonwealth parliament?" To the great amusement of the nation, Malcolm Turnbull, appearing before a joint parliamentary committee on the Referendum Bill on 5 July 1999, even tried to have the words "president" and "republic" removed from the referendum question. He wanted the question to concentrate on the term "head of state". His action was likened to Basil Fawlty's advice to staff in the BBC television series "Fawlty Towers" when a group of German tourists were to stay at his hotel: "Don't mention the war." In effect, the ARM is attempting to give the term "head of state" a constitutional meaning and application never before known in Australia. Further, it is using it as part of a contrived test by which the constitution must be judged: is an Australian our head of state?

ONLY A DIPLOMATIC TERM

The modern state emerged with the decline of feudalism in Europe. International law requires that a state must have a territory, population and government. Above all, states are juridically equal. Most were once ruled by monarchs, kings or princes, who had removed themselves from the higher authority of the Holy Roman Emperor or the Pope. Relations between states at this time essentially involved personal relations between monarchs, represented by ambassadors. The heads of those states had up to seven functions: ceremonial, religious, diplomatic, military, executive, legislative, and judicial.

With the emergence of constitutional monarchies and republics, the functions of the head of state (a term introduced to cover the few heads of republics), have tended to be reduced. They are now usually at least one of the following: ceremonial, executive, diplomatic and the constitutional umpire and auditor.

However it is not truly possible to generalise about what are or should be the functions of a head of state. This is because international law does not provide the answer. As Lord Slynn observed in *R vs Bartle (ex parte Pinochet)*, House of Lords, 25 November 1998: "The role of head of state varies very much from country to country. International law recognises those functions which are attributed to him as head of state by the law or in fact in the country of which he is head as being functions for this purpose, subject to any general principle of customary international law or national law which may prevent what is done from being regarded as a function." Or as Humpty Dumpty said: "When I use a word it means just what I choose it to mean – neither more or less."

A few heads of state still have religious functions, such as the Queen (but only as Queen of the United Kingdom of Great Britain and Northern Ireland), the Pope, and the King of Morocco. Nor can we generalise about the number of heads of state in a country or whether the head of state is a collective. Andorra had two heads of state, the Soviet Union 24, revolutionary France, under the Directory, five. A head of state can change to a monarch from being republican head and vice versa. This has happened in France, Albania, Iran and Cambodia. A head of state can be head of more than one country. And the head of state can also be the head of government, as in the United States. Some of the usual functions of the head of state can be vested in the Speaker, as in Sweden. Apart from observing that the head of state will normally rank highest in the order of precedence in a given country, there is no hard and fast rule even in determining who actually is the head of state. This is especially so in revolutionary situations, for example Chile immediately after the overthrow of President Allende.

It is an indisputable fact that the Australian government holds out and other countries accept that the governor-general is the Australian head of state. He is accorded this status by other states when he travels. So the constitutional lawyer Professor Colin Howard concludes that "... practice and law so coincide to support the proposition that, certain matters of ceremony and courtesy apart, the head of state in Australia is not the queen but the governor-general". When the Pope recently visited the United States he was welcomed by President Clinton. President Clinton as head of state ranks first in precedence in the USA, so in this respect he is similar to the governor-general. But he also is the head of government, so he is also similar to the prime minister.

Under international law and diplomatic practice a head of state came to be accorded certain courtesies, for example a 21-gun salute. Heads of state began to deal directly with one another, or through ambassadors. As heads of state are equal, no head of state could sit in judgement on another. This is expressed in the principle *par in parem non habet jurisdictionem*. For this reason, a head of state is normally immune from the jurisdiction of a foreign court, exceptions being allowed in exceptional cases, such as in the 1999 trial in England of Chile's General Pinochet for alleged human rights abuses. In the unlikely event that the Australian governor-general was charged with an ordinary offence while travelling overseas, there is not a shadow of doubt that he would be immune from the jurisdiction as our head of state.

In the common law of Australia, Canada, Britain and the United States, the term head of state is relevant *only* for international law matters and in diplomatic relations. The term is not one used or known in domestic constitutional law in those countries. To ascertain who actually is a head of state, we are normally informed by the department of foreign affairs of our country or of the foreign country. Who the head of state is – for international purposes – is always a matter for the country concerned. So is what he or she does, and what office he or she holds under the country's constitution. There is no single model. The head of state can be a king, emperor, a king-emperor, a grand duke, an elector, a prince, a president, the pope.

The head can be almost purely ceremonial (Ireland) or the head of government (USA), or a powerful executive president "cohabiting" with a parliamentary prime minister (France) or the holder of absolute power as in various dictatorships. Hitler was a head of state, but Stalin never was according to their country's constitutions.

The term "head of state" is not used as a title in most foreign constitutions. The first principal usage of the term in the twentieth century seems to have been under fascist regimes. In Spain, when the office of king was vacant, Generalissimo Franco became *Jefe d'Estado*. Similarly, Marechal Petain became *Chef de l'Etat* (as well as *President de la Republique*) in Vichy France.

To confirm that the term "head of state" is not used and completely unknown to Australian constitutional law, reference may be made to the federal and all state constitutions; the *Balfour Declaration*; the proceedings of the *Imperial Conference*, 1930 as they relate to the appointment of governors-general; the *Statute of Westminster*, 1931; the *Statute of Westminster Adoption Act*, 1942; the *Royal Powers Act*, 1953; the *Royal Style and Titles Acts*, 1953 and 1973; and the *Australia Acts*, 1986. In no section of any one of these acts will you find the term "head of state".

And just as head of state is not used in our constitutional law or practice, nor has it been a part of everyday English for very long. There is no mention of "head of state" in the many entries in the 2000-odd pages of the first edition of the *Macquarie Dictionary*, 1981. You'll find "loose-head", from rugby. And "head" meaning a ship's toilet. There's the colloquial use of the word for a drug user. "Head-hunting", "head boy" and "heading dog" are there, along-side "headmaster" and "headmistress". And under "state" there is "state aid", "state righter", the American "statehouse" (which is not to be confused it seems with the New Zealand "state house", a private dwelling built and owned by the state). There is "state-of-the-art", "statesman" and "stateswoman". But no "head of state".

If it was unknown to Australians, was it used by the Americans and not the English? Consulting a *Webster's Dictionary* of 1909 – the Australasian Edition – we find illustrations of the use of the word "head" include: "The husband is the head of the wife" as Christ is the "head of the Church" and "head of the table". But no "head of state". (There is however a "head maggot"!) And the world "state" is used in combinations such as "state rights", the continental "States General" and the historical "Papal State". But again, no reference to "head of state".

In 1998, the London *Daily Telegraph* commissioned the Gallop Organisation, to conduct an opinion poll: "Could you tell me who is head of state in the United Kingdom at the moment?" Only 56 per cent gave the correct response. Fifteen per cent thought Tony Blair was, and 27 per cent did not know. Even in the United Kingdom, where there is no debate between republicans and anti-republicans about who is head of state, there is still confusion about the term.

THE REPUBLICAN DEBATE

The ARM, and above all Prime Minister Keating, have been thrashing about for years for a respectable argument to justify a constitutional upheaval. Paul Keating had used republicanism to try to castigate the conservatives for confusing Australia's national interest with those of Britain. What would he say then to the poem Labor legend 'Doc' Evatt chose as a rallying call for a broadcast in the early part of the Second World War:

And we shall say to all the world
That kinship follows space
And he who fights the British Isles
Must fight the British race.

In introducing the term "head of state" into the debate the ARM and Mr Keating are of course vastly helped by those in the media who have decided not only that the issue is newsworthy, but that it is desirable. Public funding of the Republic Advisory Committee's (RAC) caravan around Australia helped their case, and so did postage of ARM's proposals to all citizens around Australia. Yet public interest remained low.

Insertion of the term "head of state" into dinner party conversation was never the result of some visionary plan. Rather the ARM and how Mr Keating stumbled into it. But it has proved a quite useful way to distract the people. The term is just beginning to be used in New Zealand, Canada and even the United Kingdom. And by 1997 it had actually appeared in an Australian dictionary. Dictionaries reflect usage, and the ARM had won a victory in changing the language.

The *Age* in its editorial of 24 April 1999, just before Anzac Day, lamented that the constitutional debate had been "mired in secondary disputes about how a president would be chosen". Nothing at all about the crucial question – how a president should be dismissed? "The primary question," lectured the *Age*, is "whether Australians want an Australian as head of state?" Which of course is not the question in the referendum. So the ARM's strategy in the referendum is to try to substitute Mr Keating's proposed plebiscite question for the actual referendum question.

THE GOVERNOR-GENERAL

In the Keating–Turnbull republic the powers of the governor-general, who is said not to be a head of state, are to be transferred to the president, who becomes a head of state.

Sir David Smith was private secretary to several governors-general. He is a leading authority on this office.

An extraordinary debate arose between Sir David and former Chief Justice Sir Anthony Mason who had, in a paper to the Australian National University in 1998, dismissed Sir David's argument that the governor-general is head of state as "arrant nonsense". Sir David's response, given in a paper to the Samuel Griffiths Society that year, sets out what he sees as the errors of fact and of law made by the former chief justice.

Sir Anthony had argued that section 2 of the constitution was definitive. This refers to the governor-general as the "queen's representative". But Sir David cites contrary opinions from "seven distinguished constitutional lawyers and jurists, and one governor-general who is also a distinguished constitutional lawyer". He says that the former chief justice was obviously not aware that the constitution gave the Australian governor-general an executive power not previously granted to any other governor-general in the British Empire; or that Queen Victoria's ministers were wrong in advising her to issue royal instructions to the governor-general in 1900. He continues: "Sir Anthony is obviously not aware that the Queen revoked those Instructions in 1984."

Pointing out that governors-general are accorded head of state status when travelling overseas, Sir David refers to 51 state and official visits to 33 foreign countries since 1971. (As recently as April and May 1999, Governor-General Sir William Deane was accorded head of state status when visiting Turkey and Ireland.) The former chief justice had mentioned only one such instance, and according to Sir David "gets it wrong". He had written of a supposed visit by Sir John Kerr to Iran for the coronation of the Shah. The coronation visit was in fact made by Sir Paul Hasluck in 1971; the state visit to Iran was made in 1975.

The former chief justice had also referred to the early role of the governor-general as the representative of the British government – a situation which did exist, and was changed in 1926. Sir David in fact delivered a paper on this very subject in Parliament House in 1995. He says that the change in 1926 was not as the former chief justice described it. It was not a change in the way the governor-general saw the responsibilities of his office. Rather it was a change in the way the British and the Australian ministers saw those responsibilities. The governor-general, he says, had nothing to do with it!

Sir David is of course correct. The changes made by the 1926 *Balfour Declaration* were sweeping. It changed the crown and the commonwealth. And it was made by the commonwealth prime ministers, not the governors-general.

Then the former chief justice referred to a "robust convention" that the governor-general does not attend a function in Australia when the queen herself is present. Sir David writes that such a *practice* did exist. But there was no constitutional or conventional reason for it. He agrees that the governor-general has not been present when the queen has opened the federal parliament. This, he says, is because of changes made to the standing orders of both houses of the parliament that had previously provided for the opening speech to be delivered by the governor-general. In 1953 both houses amended their standing orders to provide that, in certain circumstances, references to the governor-general should be read as references to the queen. This was done under the *Royal Powers Act* 1953 not, as the former Chief Justice says, the *Royal Style and Titles Act.*

The act allows the queen, whenever she is present in Australia, to exercise any power under an act exercisable by the governor-general. It did not prevent the governor-general from continuing to exercise his statutory powers while the queen is in Australia, and in fact governors-general have continued to do so. The representative role was reversed. The sovereign was empowered to act as a delegate of the governor-general.

The conflict between these two eminent Australians over whether there is a convention on this point came to a head in their dispute over Governor-General Sir Zelman Cowan's absence when the queen opened the high court building in Canberra in 1980. Sir David writes that he knew of no constitutional or other basis for this practice, so he took the matter up with Buckingham Palace in the course of the preparations for the 1980 royal visit. He was told that the palace knew of no basis for the practice. Indeed, it seemed to be peculiar to Australia! He was advised that the queen would be pleased if the governor-general were present when she opened the high court. Sir David then revealed the really extraordinary reason why the governor-general was not present at the opening. The prime minister decided the governor-general should not be present: "With the governor-general out of the way, his place in the official procession next to the Duke of Edinburgh would be available for the prime minister. Sir Zelman asked me not to pursue the matter, but he was disappointed and very hurt."

So there was no convention, robust or otherwise. Just a prime minister's wish to sit on the dais! When the queen opened the Commonwealth Games in Brisbane in 1982, Governor-General Sir Ninian Stephen was present and seated next to her, the governor-general of Canada was when she opened the Commonwealth Games in Edmonton in 1978 – two years before the high court opening.

THE OLYMPIC GAMES

What any head of state actually does in the office he or she holds is a matter for the law and practice of the country concerned. In Australia, who performs which ceremonial function is a matter for the government of the day to determine, although much will be left to practice. If a foreign head of state visits Australia, he is usually greeted by the governor-general. But when the Pope last visited Australia, the welcoming address was given by Prime Minister Keating. As the Pope is also the head of state of Vatican City, this was unusual. But under our law and practice, it was open to the prime minister to advise the governor-general not to deliver the address so that he might deliver it himself. Similar principles apply in relation to other ceremonies, for example opening a public building – or the Olympic Games.

Australia is undoubtedly a great sporting nation. But surely Australians are not so attached to sport that we should change our constitution simply for this event. Surely not merely so that a republican president can say, "I declare open the Games of the Sydney Olympiad." Yet this argument has been put with apparent seriousness. This must be the first Olympic Games when such a change has been proposed. What would the ancient Greeks have made of it?

The rules of the International Olympic Committee provide that the "Olympic Games shall be proclaimed open by the head of state of the host country".

A state has wide authority in deciding who is its head of state, and what are his or her functions. So when we come to ceremonial functions like the opening of the Olympic Games, it is better to describe these as "ceremonial functions of the state", rather than "ceremonial functions of the head of state".

In our relations with other states, Australia determines who exercises all such ceremonial functions. It is even more appropriate that these issues be determined by Australia in matters relating to organisations of a lesser status, particularly those having no legal personality in international law. This is not to denigrate these organisations, merely to comment on their legal status. While the president of the IOC is addressed as "Excellency", this does not determine the status of the IOC; it may be a courtesy accorded because of a former position held by the president, or it may be the practice in the IOC. Whatever the reason, it does not mean the IOC is anything more than a worthy non-governmental organisation. The president of the IOC is not therefore a head of state, nor is Australia bound to accord him the courtesies due to a head of state.

The reference to "head of state" in the IOC rules cannot be taken to refer to a particular Australian office, as there is no mention of a head of state in the Australian constitution. In the United States it was the president – the head of state and the head of government – who opened the Los Angeles Games. In a country with a *collegiate* head of state, presumably one person from the college would be selected. If we were to have no separate head of state, as the Law Council of Australia once proposed, another official would be chosen to exercise this function. The IOC rules do not mean the IOC is attempting to decide who our head of state is, something even a great power would not dare to do. Nor does it mean that the person usually recognised as our head of state is to perform this function – that is a matter for Australian law and practice. Rather the rules are in effect a request that the opening of the Games be considered a high ceremonial function of the host state.

In Australia, three office holders (or their representatives) normally exercise the highest state ceremonial functions: the Queen of Australia, the Governor-General, and the Prime Minister. The final decision or advice on these matters rests conventionally with the prime minister. This does not mean the prime minister is a head of state.

The proclamation of the opening of the Games is clearly a high ceremonial function. The determination of the appropriate office holder to perform this high function, under our constitutional conventions and practice, lies with the prime minister. His choice would normally be either the queen, the governor-general or himself.

The conclusion therefore must be that we in Australia should take the IOC rule to constitute a request to the host country to treat the opening of the Olympic Games as a high state ceremonial function. It should be performed by a person holding an office in Australia the duties of which include the performance of such ceremonial functions. Who should actually do this is a matter for the competent authority in the host country, not a matter for the IOC. It would be unacceptable for a foreign power to direct or advise us on these matters. It would be inconceivable that any international non-state association would seek to do this.

The determining authority in these matters under Australian law and practice is the prime minister. Accordingly, it is entirely proper for the prime minister to open the Sydney Olympic Games.

4
THE AUSTRALIAN CROWN

The crown is not just one person, however superbly Queen Elizabeth II has filled her role as sovereign.

It is in the name of the crown that governments are carried on, laws made and justice dispensed. It is to the crown that the loyalty – and the non-political nature – of the armed forces is sworn. Central to our constitutional system, it is the method whereby representative government, responsible to parliament, can both be ensured and kept within its proper limits. Its purpose now is to protect the people and the institutions against abuse. It mandates a pattern of behaviour for the heads of our federal commonwealth and those of the state. And it is a link between our past, our present and our future. As philosopher Edmund Burke observed: "Society is indeed a contract. It becomes a partnership not only between those who are living, but between those who are dead, and those who are to be born." The crown has been with us since 1788. Rather than being foreign, it is as Australian as our laws, our parliaments, our Australian democracy itself. The crown, our oldest political institution, along with English and the rule of law, is as Australian as our beaches and our forests.

THE CONSTITUTIONAL UMPIRE AND AUDITOR

The crown of Australia, and the crown of New Zealand, the crown of Canada and the other crowns have all developed from a single imperial crown, which is now the crown of the United

Kingdom of Great Britain and Northern Ireland. There are now seventeen crowns, with Elizabeth II as sovereign of each.

But the crown of Australia is as different from the British crown as the Australian versions of the common law, parliament, and the language are different from the British versions.

The crown of Australia consists, at its pinnacle, of eight offices: the sovereign, the governor-general and the state governors. These offices guard the exercise of wide executive and legislative powers, but not for the personal use or benefit of the incumbents. Nor are these powers exercised to advance any policies that they as individuals may wish to pursue. They are not offices filled by politicians, although the incumbent may have *retired* from politics. And it is not so much the powers the crown exercises that are important. It is the powers the crown denies others.

As guardians and trustees for the people of executive power, the governor-general and the governors act to protect the public interest. The beneficiaries of their guardianship are the people, not the politicians.

In the exercise of these offices, the incumbents normally act on advice. In the nineteenth century, the noted authority on the British constitution, Walter Bagehot, defined the traditional rights of the constitutional monarch as the right to be consulted, the right to encourage, and the right to warn.

In performing their duties the incumbents are guided by convention – unwritten customs or practices that are rules of constitutional morality. These are considered binding, but the general view is that they are not enforceable by the courts. One of the faults of the Keating–Turnbull republic is that these conventions may be enforceable and reviewable in the courts. The result could be that a constitutional crisis could drag on for months, of political – and financial – instability, as we have seen in recent years in Pakistan.

This system reflects the accumulated wisdom of the extraordinary civilisation that we have inherited. It provides for leadership beyond politics, is a check and balance against the abuse of the power. So apart from a ceremonial and unifying role, the governor-general and the governors exercise the role of constitutional referee or umpire, as we saw in 1975 when the governor-general dismissed the prime minister, and as the governor of New South Wales did in 1932 when he believed the government had breached the law. In Queensland in November 1987, it seemed unlikely that Governor Sir Walter Campbell would agree to Premier Bjelke-Petersen forming a new government when he was unlikely to have retained the confidence of the Legislative Assembly.

In June 1989 the Tasmanian governor (Sir Philip Bennett) and in March 1991 the New South Wales governor (Rear Admiral Peter Sinclair) played significant roles in commissioning minority governments. On 3 September 1998, Tasmanian Governor Sir Guy Green's official secretary issued a press release to quell calls for the governor to swear in a new premier immediately. He could not do this until the polls had been declared and the writs certified.

Governors-general or governors also act as constitutional auditors. They require that the advice they receive proposes action that is lawful, that due process has been observed.

The governor first needs to know what precisely he or she is being asked to do, and then needs to be satisfied that he or she has the power to do this. The identification of the source of power leads to the question of whether there are any conditions prescribed on the exercise of the power. If the answer is yes, as it usually is, the governor needs to be satisfied that those conditions have been satisfied.

The almost daily chore of acting as auditor usually escapes the public gaze. Many people in ministerial offices and the public service are well aware of this role, yet surprisingly few commentators write of it, or even know of it. It does surface sometimes when the politicians are irritated by a governor merely because he insists on due process, or when the public becomes involved in community action.

In March 1999, for instance, the governor of New South Wales asked for a detailed briefing from the Department of

Gaming before authorising 18 governor's liquor licences over crown land at the Fox Studios Moore Park film studio and entertainment complex that replaced Sydney's old show ground. The Centennial Park Residents' Association had petitioned the governor requesting his personal intervention.

According to his official secretary, the governor wished to be satisfied that the residents' concerns had been considered and proper processes followed (*Sydney Morning Herald*, 25 March 1999). He said that such a briefing was not unusual but "doesn't happen every day". The governor then called a meeting of the executive council, at which the licences were granted. A spokesperson for the residents' association said they were heartened that the governor had taken a "serious and conscientious personal consideration of the issues raised".

If the 1999 referendum is approved, section 59 of the *Australian Constitution* will remove any similar role from the governor-general, although such a drastic move was not even contemplated in the model that emerged with less than majority support from the 1998 Constitutional Convention.

Of the two mainland territories, only the Northern Territory has adopted the Westminster system. The Australian Capital Territory actually functions without a constitutional umpire or auditor.

The dangers of this were pointed out in a letter from Neil James published in the *Canberra Times* in June 1999 under the title "Bruce fiasco a warning against republicanism". It related to concerns about whether proper authorisation had been given to the Bruce Stadium, a major project undertaken by the ACT government.

The letter argued that the "funding fiasco" would probably not have occurred in any proper Westminster system. He pointed out that if the ACT had had an impartial administrator with reserve powers and responsibilities (like the Northern Territory) he or she would have refused to sign the relevant executive council minute authorising the "expenditure" or the "loan" without further legal advice from the solicitor-general. He gave examples of this, suggesting that the absence of this control was the reason why republicans want to remove such tried and tested supra-political protection from the whole country.

The role of constitutional referee or umpire involves the exercise of what is sometimes called the "reserve powers". They are not a set of legal powers as such. Rather the phrase refers to the personal exercise of a power by a governor-general or governor who acts on his or her own discretion to resolve a crisis, or perhaps just a vacuum in government. It may relate to the appointment or dismissal of a government, or the granting of a dissolution of the parliament. In such exceptional cases the governor-general or governor is not bound to act on the advice of the executive council, the prime minister or the premier. The point is that the constitutional system must be such that it can deal with crises effectively, promptly, and democratically. The person exercising this power must be impartial and above politics.

Australia is one of the handful of countries that has a constitution that has been able to provide such safeguards over an extended period.

The sovereign is at the centre of this delicately balanced system. It is the sovereign who, on advice, appoints the governor-general and the governors.

Importantly, it is to the sovereign and through her to the people that the governor-general and the governors owe their allegiance and duty. Not to a mere politician. When India's Prime Minister Indira Ghandi sought in 1975 to impose an unjustifiable declaration of an emergency in order to avoid the consequences of a court ruling against her, the president hesitated. Mrs Ghandi reminded the president that she and the Congress Party had "made" him. It was to the party and to her that he owed his position and his loyalty. No sovereign had appointed him. He signed. No Australian governor-general or governor would have. Their loyalty and their allegiance is to the sovereign and thus to the people.

This was demonstrated clearly in 1951 when Prime Minister Menzies sought a double dissolution that many in the Labor

Party thought would be blocked by Governor-General Sir William McKell. Had he not been a Labor premier, would he not continue to be loyal to the party and avoid an inconvenient election? In fact he disregarded any feeling of loyalty to his party and, acting according to convention, granted the double dissolution.

The crown has developed to encompass a complex set of relations, offices, and conventions. As such it has been defended vigorously by all of the Canadian provincial governments, both English and French-speaking.

When the Canadian government proposed legislative changes in 1978 that would have made the governor-general dismissible on the advice of the federal cabinet, the provincial premiers met and issued a communiqué endorsed unanimously by all ten, including Quebec:

Provinces agree that the system of democratic parliamentary government requires an ultimate authority to ensure its responsible nature and to safeguard against abuses of power. That ultimate power must not be an instrument of the federal cabinet. The Premiers, therefore, *oppose constitutional changes that substitute for the Queen as ultimate authority*, a governor-general whose appointment and dismissal would be solely at the pleasure of the federal cabinet. (Heard, 43)

In 1996, the Premier of Quebec declared that the "monarchy is the last bulwark of democracy". Canadian Prime Minister Jean Chretien pointed out that although "the American Revolution was promoted by the French, the Quebecois felt more secure with the monarchy". (Handley and Holloway 16, 17)

All of the officers of the crown – the sovereign, the governor-general and the governors – normally act on advice. But there may still be a residue of royal power, where there is some personal discretion. While the emphasis is usually on the governor-general and governors, the sovereign herself may still enjoy some undefined discretion to maintain the integrity of the system. Thus, where inappropriate proposals have been suggested in relation to the office of governor-general – that it be filled by a committee, or for more than a temporary period by the chief justice – the sovereign has let it be known that formal advice along these lines should not be tendered. (Bogdanor, 284–285)

Those who think that the queen is an automaton underestimate the subtlety of the system, as well as the integrity and ability of our sovereign. It is worth recalling the queen's role in the two Fijian military coups. She sent two messages to the governor-general, both as Queen of Fiji. Most importantly, both were made without ministerial advice. This was because she refused to recognise the authority of the new military government. One message was a declaration that the governor-general remained the sole source of executive authority. She expressed the hope that the process of restoring the country to constitutional normality might be resumed. Later, after the second coup, she acknowledged that the governor-general was unable to preserve constitutional government and had to resign. She said she was sad to think the ending of Fijian allegiance to the crown should have been brought about without the Fijian people being given the opportunity to express their feelings on the proposal. (Bogdanor, 287) In 1999, it was revealed that queen had in fact played a key role in saving Fiji from falling apart. According to the then permanent secretary to the governor-general, her "moral and legal backing" of him was crucial. (*Courier Mail*, 29 April 1999; Thomson 159, 160)

THE SECOND KEATING–TURNBULL REPUBLIC

Can this delicately balanced structure be replaced by grafting the second Keating–Turnbull republic on to the constitution? Remember that what is being proposed is not some vague idea of a republic, but a specific model. Wisely, the founders of the constitution insisted that anyone proposing change detail the specific changes to the people at, and not after, the referendum.

The Keating–Turnbull republic would first split the crown into seven crowns – the federal and six state crowns. This would be a dangerous step if there were the secessionist pressures of previous years.

This division goes against received constitutional doctrine, the crown having only been divided previously to allow for the total independence of the original realms or dominions.

The proposal then is to republicanise Australia by a piecemeal approach. The states will of course be secondary targets for change, as well as the flag, the armed services, the currency and whatever is next on the agenda.

The proposal for change at first only at the federal level is extraordinary. It is to dismantle one seventh of the crown of Australia. Although the 1998 Constitutional Convention communiqué recommended that the powers of the governor-general flow to the president, it seems that the governor-general's day-to-day role as constitutional auditor could disappear under the proposed section 59. He *must* then act only on advice. His role as constitutional referee could be supervised by the high court. And under the proposed republic the prime minister can dismiss him (and any acting president). This is so despite the fact that the Republic Advisory Committee, created by Paul Keating and chaired by Malcolm Turnbull, reported almost universal opposition to a provision such as this, which would mean the president holds office "at the whim of the prime minister".

As former minister Reg Withers says, it will be easier for the prime minister to sack the president than his driver.

Under this republic, unlike the present system that has ensured governors-general and governors give leadership above politics, the politicians must do a deal to choose the president. That is the result of the requirement for election by a two-thirds vote of a joint sitting of parliament. It imposes, indeed entrenches, deal-making. We shall probably not know the trade-offs involved in any deal, just as we had no knowledge of the Kirribilli House agreement between Bob Hawke and Paul Keating, witnessed only by Bill Kelty and Sir Peter Abeles, to hand over the prime ministership after the 1990 election. We only learned about it when Bob Hawke changed his mind and it was leaked.

DEFENDERS OF THE CROWN

There are two broad groups of people who will argue the No case at the 1999 referendum. First there are those who in principal are in favour of changing to a republic, but are dissatisfied with the model. They understand that this republic consolidates the politicians' hold on power. (The fact is that one can oppose this republic, but still be a republican.) Secondly, there are people who sincerely believe that the Australian system of constitutional monarchy offers arrangements superior to any that may be offered by a republican system.

We cannot of course generalise about the nature of these constitutionalists or the reasons for their views. The initiating instrument for the community lobby group Australians for Constitutional Monarchy declares in its *Charter for the Defence of the Australian Constitution*:

We are Australians united to defend our constitutional system of government. As befits a free people living in a parliamentary democracy, there are amongst us differences of view and emphasis:

* Some of us support the system [believing] it is the least imperfect form of government yet devised and it should endure in Australia indefinitely.
* Some of us, whilst willing to contemplate the possibility of a different form of government at some future time, oppose the attempt to raise such a debate at this time . . .
* Some of us believe that Australia is already a form of republic under the crown: a "crowned republic". Australia enjoys all the desirable features of a republican government and a constitutional monarchy without any disadvantages of either system . . .
* Some of us simply admire Her Majesty the Queen of Australia. We are hurt and angry at the attacks on her in recent times despite her exemplary lifetime of service to her people.

The charter is reproduced at the back of *The Australian Constitutional Monarchy* edited by G. Grainger and K. Jones.

Until 1975, members of the political and judicial establishment rarely, if ever, espoused republicanism. That has since changed.

Mr Justice Michael Kirby is renowned for his interest in legal reform. That he is also a constitutional monarchist is seen by some as at least worthy of comment.

He has explained that while he supports reform of society and its laws, "reform means more than change. It means change for the better. My proposition is that the establishment of a Federal Republic of Australia would not be a change for the better."

He says arguments such as Asian conceptions of Australian identity are unacceptable as reasons for changing to a republic. He acknowledges that for some in Asia the concept of Queen Elizabeth II as Queen of Australia may be difficult to grasp. Yet, he says, there are niceties of the constitutions of the monarchies of Japan, Thailand and Malaysia – not to say of the republics of the region – that we do not fully understand.

No self-respecting country should abandon its history and institutions out of deference to the misunderstandings of its neighbours. No country should alter its constitutional arrangements, if they work well, simply because neighbouring countries do not fully appreciate its history or understand its independence. Regional comity has not, nor should it, come to this.

He suggests that people of his generation, who have witnessed at least two reigns, are impressed by the personal example set by the sovereign, and the sense of continuity the institution provides. The sovereign can provide a personal symbol of constitutional continuity. In a fast-changing world, some items of continuity – and the institutions which protect them – provide reassurance and stability.

The sovereign, Kirby contends, must in modern times be held in high esteem if the system is to endure. He concedes that the saga of crises in the royal family have had detrimental effects on the standing of the institution, despite the continued admiration for the queen. But Kirby cautions us to see them in perspective. The crises of 1993 he says, will inevitably fade in public memory.

In considering republicanism, Australians will see – in increasingly stark relief – the continuity of the service of their queen. He rejects criticisms of Australians' apparent reluctance to agree to constitutional change.

For example, he says it would now be generally accepted that the rejection of the Menzies government's referendum in 1951 to dissolve the Australian Communist Party was an important protection of civil liberties in Australia. But, Kirby reminds us, at the beginning of the campaign polls showed that 80 per cent of the people were in favour. When it came to the vote, only three states voted in favour. The national affirmative vote was 49.44 per cent. He argues that the requirement in our constitution that the people agree to change in a referendum has been a wonderful guarantee of our freedoms.

Moving to arguments of principle, Kirby says that the present wave of republicanism has strong connotations of nineteenth-century nationalism which he, characteristically, argues should be rejected in favour of internationalism. Since Hiroshima, he says, intelligent people should abhor nationalism and seek international harmony. The sovereign is an international one, and none the worse for that fact. The idea that we must have a local head of state always resident in our midst, is one that derives from an inflexibility of mind. It has been superseded by modern telecommunications, the jumbo jet and global ideas.

Kirby believes that our constitutional monarchy presents a tempering force against narrow nationalism. It softens brutal majoritarianism by providing an ultimate symbolism.

He continues his attack on nationalism by making reference to our relationship with New Zealand, an argument that could (to a lesser degree) also be applied to other regional neighbours including Papua New Guinea and the Solomon Islands. He believes that we must keep in mind the utility of our sharing a constitutional monarch with that close neighbour in our region. We should pause before severing such a special link with the country closest to our history and identity.

Kirby points out that under our present system, because of an accident of history and birth, the sovereign can and should aspire to no such political role or power. Nor should – or do – her representatives. The same may not be true if we alter the incumbent and the method of determining the incumbency.

Kirby argues for the benefits of our system as a constitutional compromise. He says we have in Australia, in all truth, a "crowned republic". We have the advantages of constitutional monarchy, as practised in so many peaceful democracies. We have the historical symbols of a constitutional system of a thousand years without the trappings of aristocracy and other features that would be inimical to Australian public life. And yet he says we avoid the pretensions to which a home grown republic could easily succumb. In fact, we have developed in Australia a mature system in which, although we have the queen and the governor-general and governors, we are mercifully free of the pompositics that elsewhere accompany local heads of state.

AN INFLEXIBLE MONARCHY?

One of the great strengths of our constitution is that it is not formalised and therefore it is capable of adaptation and evolution. A frequent criticism that is often levelled against the monarchy is that it is archaic, rigid and inflexible.

The British authority on constitutional monarchy Vernon Bogdanor, explains that this is not the case at all. He argues that whereas the American presidency has changed little since the time of George Washington, the English monarchy of the late twentieth century would be virtually unrecognisable to a contemporary of George III.

American Professor Daniel Lazar has compared the "crowned republic" of Great Britain with the system of the United States. He points out that the United Kingdom has no supreme court to serve as a restraint on government, no formal bill of rights, and a parliament that, if it wanted to, could wipe out civil liberties at a stroke.

The curious thing is that it does not. Rather, the United States has, he says, a poorer record. Ever since Margaret Thatcher's rise to power in the late seventies, British liberals have been bemoaning the damage done to civil liberties by right-wing governments. From an American perspective, he says, these need to be taken with a grain of salt. Just as the levels of crime in the most economically depressed British neighbourhoods hardly compare to crime in Detroit or the South Bronx, civil liberties violations simply do not compare with what Americans are used to on almost a daily basis. While British civil libertarians were up in arms over the methods used to impede mass picketing in the 1984–85 coal miners' strike, such methods were in a different league from the mass firings and arrests that the Reagan administration used to crush the air traffic controllers' strike in 1981. Lazar agrees that the prosecutions of journalists for violations of Britain's *Official Secrets Act* were a scandal. But they do not compare to the American treatment of a range of dissidents from Mark Hampton, the Black Panther who died in a fusillade of police gunfire in Chicago in 1969, to the Branch Davidians, 81 of whom, he says, needlessly perished in a federal assault in 1993.

He argues that despite the absence of a bill of rights and judicial review, the British somehow did not gaol thousands of radicals after World War I. Nor did they make hundreds of thousands of arrests as part of the prohibition of alcohol; harass thousands of accused communists in the forties and fifties; or arrest millions in the drug war. Nor did the Canadians, the Australians or the New Zealanders. The Americans did. Britain and America, he says, share a common history, "yet something about makeup, their construction, causes them to function according to very different principles". Surely that is the British (and Australian) constitutional system?

AN AUSTRALIAN CROWN EMERGES

A separate Australian crown gradually emerged earlier this century. This was formally recognised by the Australian parliament in the *Royal Titles Act*, 1953 and 1973.

Speaking in 1973 minister Kim Beazley senior said:

I believe that there is one remaining function and a very important remaining function of the Monarchy; that it is a focal point of allegiance. If the wielders of practical political power also become the focal point of allegiance, then they can become very dangerous. Hitler was an example of a person who both wielded practical political power and was the focal point of allegiance. In so far as the Monarchy therefore is the focal point of allegiance without wielding practical political power, it acts as a lightning conductor; it stops the people who are wielding political power assuming that they are permanent. The permanency in the Constitution is in the crown.

... I agree that this [the passing of ...] is an occasion the significance of which should be noted. It is an assertion of the separateness of the crown of Australia, the distinctiveness of the crown of Australia and the concept of a crown acting on the advice of the Australian Government. We rarely, of course, have dealings directly with the person of the Monarch. The representative is the governor-general. But this is an appropriate assertion of Australia's nationhood at this time. (Beazley, K., "Hansard", House of Representatives, 23 August 1973, p 358)

Kim Beazley senior's comment that permanence in the constitution derives from the crown has been developed by Justice Kirby, who points out that he and other high officials – judges, ministers, politicians, police, defence forces – are citizens cast by our system into the state of mind that they all are merely temporary office-holders *under* the crown. This, he says, puts a break on "any delusions of grandeur" and a check on arbitrary power. Because the sovereign "serves, here as elsewhere, in a line which can be traced back a thousand years, [this] puts a brake on the temptation to a *coup d'état* or to a breach of valid constitutional conventions". He warns that this virtue might, or might not, pass to a new republic. The very continuity of constitutional monarchy is a symbolic assurance against the brutal assertion of oppressive power, and it is one ingredient for tolerance and diversity – whereas the symbols of a republic may fall into the "trap of democratic majoritarianism".

Kim Beazley senior draws on the theme of a focal point of allegiance aloof from political power. Twenty-five years later his old political opponent Sir James Killen spoke in similar terms in the same chamber of the unifying force of the crown, echoing the words of the English essayist Walter Bagehot. Killen said that the dominant feature of the crown has been the uniting influence in the federation. "You cannot disturb that without destroying the federation." He reminded Australians that "this country is divided by politics and by party. The crown is of no party, of no division and of no conflict. Reflect on that, and I think you will come with me and walk along the road to support the status quo". (*Report of the Constitutional Convention*, 2–13 February 1998, Vol. 3, p 266)

A common allegiance to the crown was a critical unifying force in the years leading up to federation, overcoming fierce colonial loyalties and differences ranging from football rules to train-track sizes. Allegiance to the crown transcended all of this.

MANY CROWNS

This institution has an uncanny ability to unify. This is the case even in Papua New Guinea where, as former Prime Minister Michael Somare explains, despite the lack of any ancient or racial connection between the monarchy and the people:

People in my country feel the Queen represents the common bond that holds us together ... people see in her someone who is above tribal loyalty and conflict. (McDonald, 62)

He continues:

When the time came for us to discuss the course our constitutional development should take, we went around and sought out people's views. They all said they wanted to have the Queen as head of state.

It is doubtful whether the people actually used the term "head of state". What they indicated, no doubt, was they wanted the queen as their queen.

The eminent Canadian constitutional authority Senator

Eugene Forsey provides a staunch defence of the place of the crown within the Canadian constitution. The significance to Australia is that Forsey brings out the place and symbolism of the crown within a federation: "The Queen is Queen of Canada, not Queen of Ontario, Queen of Quebec, Queen of British Columbia, etc. She is, of course, Queen in *all* these provinces. But her title is Queen of Canada, and it is as such that she is Queen in each of the provinces."

It is true that the details of the Australian and Canadian systems differ, but Forsey's assertion is relevant to Australia. He alerts us to the fact that the crown is a national and indivisible institution. The process proposed in the November 1999 referendum – to leave the states as monarchies in a federal republic – runs counter to this.

Forsey suggests two general assumptions underlying republicanism. First, there is the fact that, especially after the Second World War, republics have again become the fashion. Secondly, he explains, some Canadians seem to have got it into their heads that people who live in a republic are somehow "freer" than those who live in a constitutional monarchy.

That proposition is not substantiated empirically. Sir Robert Menzies also found this argument being put in Australia. He rejected it, explaining that the creation of a republic could not make complete independence more independent. He said that although a member of a republic is no more free than a subject of the queen, he may be disposed to think that he is. "He will tell his neighbours so. His neighbours will in due course come to agree with him."

Forsey's most significant argument is one that rejects the proposition that a republic would somehow be more Canadian. Just as no part of Australia has ever been a republic or part of a republic, neither has any part of Canada. To become one would be an abrupt break with the history of either country. "Our monarchy, our British monarchy, our Anglo-French monarchy, our historic monarchy", is part, he says, of the Canadian tradition. It is "bone of our bone, flesh of our flesh". (Forsey, 23)

THE CROWN AND THE PEOPLE

The Australian political scientist Professor Graham Maddox finds in the link between monarchies something that is particularly Australian. He points to a work by Patricia Springborg who has researched issues relating to republicanism. She outlined the legacy of welfare that the crown has bequeathed to the monarchical state. In medieval times the throne was retained only as long as the people were adequately protected and provided for. In primitive times, the king would provide a link to the gods. If he lost favour with the gods, the crops would fail or natural disasters would descend upon the people. The king's role, carried forward to medieval times, was to care for his people. Maddox says that Springborg's most startling conclusion – obvious once it is thought about – is that "the modern states with the strongest commitment to communal welfare are those which retained their monarchies into the twentieth century". While nobody would now expect the monarch personally to engage in welfare provision, the tradition of welfare engendered by the monarchy runs deep in the national psyche.

Maddox argues that the Australian colonies provided a kind of laboratory example for royal welfare. He rejects the view that European Australia began as a "prison" and that the first governors were "despots". In fact, their competence was restricted and subjected to close scrutiny from London. And they were on the whole men of the Enlightenment. They took on their commission with an optimistic outlook about the possibilities of social experimentation and in dealing with "uncivilised" peoples.

The colonial governors, Maddox believes, made important practical contributions to the art of government in an enlightened era. And, as historian Alan Atkinson and Professor Henry Reynolds have pointed out, in some respects the coming of responsible government actually retarded this enlightened approach. Maddox points to their policies toward the Aboriginal population, toward the management of the land, toward the treatment of ex-convicts. These were usually more advanced than those of the free settlers.

In addition, monarchies seem to have a better track record in governmental honesty. The Berlin-based international organisation Transparency Independence, which campaigns against corruption, issued a "corruption perception index" in 1998. The five most corrupt of 85 countries were all republics. Of the five least corrupt, four (Denmark, Sweden, New Zealand and Canada) were monarchies: two have Elizabeth II as their sovereign. In the 1999 United Nations Human Development Index, eight of the top ten countries are monarchies, all the least-developed ten are republics. A research survey on good government at Harvard and the University of Chicago found seven of the top ten governments were monarchies, and four had Elizabeth II as sovereign. It is clear that of the world's freest, fairest and wealthiest democracies, monarchies are the most numerous by far.

THE AUSTRALIAN CROWN AND IMMIGRATION

But if the crown is so entrenched in Australia's history, has it not been terminally weakened by immigration from outside the British Isles?

Forsey deals with the identical question of how Canadians of non-British descent can claim that the monarchy is "flesh of their flesh". It is clear that British Canadians got their ideas of constitutional government from Britain. But where did the French Canadians get their ideas? From France? From Rome? From the United States? From the Laurentian Shield or the Aurora Borealis or the waters of the St Lawrence or the Saguenay, or their own inner consciousness, or subconsciousness? No. Just as definitely as the British Canadians, they got their ideas of constitutional government from Britain; "just as plainly, as definitely and as unmistakably as they got their Civil Law from France". (Forsey, 23, 24)

Of course the monarchy does have a British connotation. But it is not the connotation of an "English woman". Rather, it is the connotation of a British system of government, developed in Britain and exported from Britain, which the constitutionalist seeks to preserve. And it is from this system that virtually all Australians draw their conception of democratic, parliamentary government. With the exception of those advocating an executive presidency, this continues to be the source of the dominant political theory in Australia. So the monarchy is as much a fundamental Australian institution as in Canada – both for those of British stock and all the other immigrants.

Forsey acknowledges the contribution immigrants from various countries have made to the Canadian constitution to which they adapted on arrival and under which they subsequently worked and prospered as citizens. He accepts that they, like any other Canadians, may encourage constitutional reform, including a republic. He is emphatic, however, that it must be done for the right reasons – not because it is "foreign" or "un-Canadian". He says: "Our monarchy is part of our Constitution; our Constitution is part of our history, which has shaped our character as a people. To get rid of it is to change that character." (Forsey, 24–25)

These words could equally refer to Australia.

5

THE AUSTRALIAN CONSTITUTIONAL SYSTEM

When the word "constitution" is used in Australia, it is often assumed that the reference is to a single document, the federal or commonwealth *Constitution* of 1901. It is not well known, for *at least* two reasons. Apart from persuading fellow Australians of the good sense of federation, the founders had to struggle neither for independence nor to overthrow an oppressive regime. And as a sensible person doesn't fiddle with a watch or a car that works superbly, there is little need for Australians to refer to it, except of course, for specialist lawyers. In fact, the constitution, broadly defined, is not contained in one single document. There is the Federal Constitution. And each state has a constitution. Then there is the *Statute of Westminster* and the *Australia Act*. And then there are the conventions, or customs, according to which certain powers are exercised.

The constitution is in fact all this and more.

Viscount Bolingbroke, some three centuries ago, defined the constitution as:

... that assembly of laws, institutions and customs, derived from certain fixed principles of reason ... that compose the general system, according to which the community has agreed to be governed.

And Australians, more than any other people, have freely and openly agreed to be governed by our constitutional system. Both the agreement to federate, and the changing of at least the federal and most of the state constitutions, is done by the people directly.

The Australian constitution of 1901 created a new political entity, but it did so in the context of several autonomous self-governing communities which had already developed out of the British colonies of settlement. These colonies had already developed strong democratic traditions, in most cases over half a century. They had embraced the Westminster system in which governments are responsible to parliament. The new constitution built on these ideas but also introduced federalism, as developed in the American constitution.

It is only if this context is considered that the development of Australia to full nationhood status can be properly understood. This is equally true of the evolving nature of the crown into a fully Australian institution – a subtle concept that has continued to develop freely within the framework of a rigid constitution. This phenomenon has been possible because of the role of unwritten conventions or customs and, also the changing relationship between Australia and the United Kingdom.

AUTONOMOUS SELF-GOVERNING COMMUNITIES DEVELOP OUT OF THE COLONIES OF SETTLEMENT

Initially the power of the colonial governor was restricted only by the law and by instructions from London. This power was later tempered by an advisory legislative council and executive council. Gradually the legislative council took on an increasingly representative flavour and, within a surprisingly short period, the executive became responsible to that legislature. This is even more remarkable if we remember that most of the states started as penal colonies. The eminent constitutional authority Professor Lane sees an analogy with seventeenth-century England where "the people had gradually wrested from the crown the power to make law and the power to raise taxes and expend public money". (Lane, 193)

Lane explains that for the first 35 years the NSW governors "ruled like local monarchs". But they did so strictly under the law they brought with them. The governor legislated, adjudicated and governed: "You should appreciate there was no local legislature or, until 1814, no supreme court, no executive council – none of these restraining institutions." The governor imposed taxation, established and interfered with law courts, civil as well as criminal, took appeals, appointed civil servants, handed out land grants and maintained an armed force, not just for defence but also for law and order. (Lane, 160) Fortunately, most governors ruled for the benefit of and interests of the people. There is little evidence of corruption or the desire for personal gain.

The passing of the *New South Wales Act*, 1823 (4 Geo IV, ch 96) transformed the penal settlement into a civil colony by establishing a legislative council consisting of crown nominees to advise, though not over-rule, the governor. The council was invested with the power "to make laws . . . for the peace, welfare, and good government" of the colony. This formula continues to be used in relation to the state parliaments' legislative powers. The high court has determined these or similar words to be the formula used by the imperial parliament when it wished to confer the plenary power exercised at Westminster on a colonial legislature: *Union Steamship Co. of Australia Pty Ltd v King*, (1988) 166 CLR 1. This broad power is in contrast to that which was to be vested in the commonwealth parliament, which was to be a legislature of specific enumerated powers. The colonial parliaments were prohibited from legislating repugnantly to the law of England – a restriction which lingered at the state level until the passing of the *Australia Acts*, 1986. The 1823 act also established the Supreme Courts of New South Wales and Van Diemen's land, with general jurisdiction over "all pleas . . . and jurisdiction in all cases whatsoever . . . [just as in Her] Majesty's Courts . . . at Westminster". Such power continues to be exercised by the state Courts.

Further reform came in 1825 with the inception of an executive council appointed to advise the governor, who remained free to depart from such advice.

The great colony founded by Governor Phillip in 1788 was

broken into four lesser colonies with the creation of Van Diemen's land in 1825, Victoria in 1851 and Queensland in 1859. Separate colonies were established in Western Australia and the Province of South Australia. Each colony in time developed similar institutions of government.

The provisions of the Imperial Act of 1823 were further enhanced by the *Australian Courts Act*, 1828 (Geo IV, ch 83), allowing the local courts to apply all the laws and statutes then in force in England and simultaneously allowing such laws to be locally amended (though this did not extend to statutes operating by paramount force until the passing of the *Australia Acts*, 1986). The act also increased the size of the legislative council.

In 1842 the first signs of representative government emerged with the passing, by the imperial parliament, of "An Act for the Government of New South Wales and Van Diemen's Land" or the *Australian Constitutions Act* No. 1, 1842 (5 & 6 vic, ch 76) allowing for two-thirds of the 36 members of the legislative council to be directly elected. A minority of members were still nominated, qualification for voting rested on stipulated property ownership, emancipists were prohibited from voting, and the governor still controlled the executive. Nevertheless, Lane sees this as a great turning point.

He says that we can identify three basic constitutional doctrines expressly found in the 1842 Act. "No taxation without representation": that is, the newly constituted people's institution was to make laws, including the tax laws. "The financial initiative of the crown": that is, the governor must first recommend to the legislature the purpose for which public money was to be appropriated. "Parliament controls the expenditure of public money": that is, an appropriation of (most) revenue must be made by the legislature, and in no other manner.

The second *Australian Constitutions Act*, 1850, "An Act for the better Government of Her Majesty's Australian Colonies", (13 & 14 Vic, ch 59) brought similar reforms to the other colonies (except for the Moreton Bay district – Queensland – which was attached to the New South Wales legislative council until 1859). This act was extremely important. It empowered the various colonies to draft their own constitutions, although they were still to be approved by the Colonial Office in London before being presented for the Queen's assent. Thus the documents that were to become the state constitutions were, as Lane puts it, "essentially home grown; even if monitored by the Imperial authorities". (Lane, 194) They were *never* imposed by London. And this was half a century before the federal constitution. In each of these cases, the constitutions for the Australian states provided for a bicameral legislature. At least the lower house was elective and the beginnings of a cabinet system of responsible government emerged. This was to mean that each of the crown's advisers were ministers of state sitting in the legislature, thus rendering the executive answerable to parliament.

Lane observes that the development of the legislative council in each of the colonies brought about constitutional monarchy in Australia.

In time it became wholly elective. It progressively took over power to make laws and raise taxes.

Lane stresses that ours is a *constitutional* monarchy, a system of government in which the crown does not exercise absolute power, only limited power under the constitution. In particular the crown is advised by its ministers who are answerable, through parliament, to the people. (Lane, 193)

The state governors survive as living symbols of the process of evolution from rule to representative and responsible government under the crown, and as constitutional umpires and auditors.

FEDERATION

When the colonies sought to federate, a written constitution was obviously needed. Such a discrete document did not regulate the affairs of the United Kingdom, nor would one regulate New Zealand when she was granted dominion status. Unlike New Zealand, Australia was to be a federation comprising six pre-existing entities and one new one. Thus it was necessary, as was the case in the United States and Canada, for a document to formally stipulate what powers the existing entities were giving up and the conditions upon which they were prepared to do so. The two main concerns of the founders are set out in the *Commonwealth of Australia Constitution Act*, 1900, an act of the imperial (British) parliament passed at the request of the Australian colonies. First, the division of powers between the new commonwealth and the existing colonies, which were to become the states of Australia. Second, the separation of powers granted to the commonwealth between its three principle organs of government: the parliament, the executive and the judiciary. Although the new federal entity was to operate on the Westminster system, in answering these two questions the founders looked to North America.

The two choices open were the American model, which allowed the states to retain considerable power, and the Canadian model, which set out powers within the control of the states and the central government but stipulated that any residual powers fell to the central government. An approach similar to the USA's was chosen on this point. Yet many were reluctant for the states to cede even this much power to the central government. The federal nature of the commonwealth also required arrangements similar to the more rigid separation of powers adopted by the Americans. This is not found in formal English laws, but in practice there is respect for the spirit of such a separation. A rigid separation between executive and judicial functions was necessary as the high court was to play a special role in the new commonwealth. It was to arbitrate between the central governments and the state government in the interpretation of the constitution. Therefore the court, and the lesser federal judiciary that was to develop later, could not be too closely associated with the federal executive.

But the rigid distinction in America between legislative and executive functions had no attraction for the founders. (Perhaps they feared that the American system would never prove to be successful when it was exported. If so, their fears have been justified.) They preferred to retain the Westminster system of responsible government that had grown up in the colonies and to which they had become accustomed. This meant that government would be formed on the floor of the lower house, as it had been in Canada. Lane recalls that the American founders wanted a thorough separation of powers, which was not acceptable to the Australians. In the United States the judiciary is separate, as with us. But the administration is also separate from the legislature, unlike us. Moreover, at the time of federation in Australia, the US had not long before endured a civil war. Civil rights were less protected there than in Australia which was a more democratic society. Theirs was not a sufficiently attractive model. On the other hand, responsible government in the British style prevailed in the Empire, and was being copied in much of continental Europe. That is why our founders kept the Westminster system under the crown.

The founders had before them an example of a Westminster republic with a president chosen by parliament – in most cases by a two-thirds majority. This was the French Third Republic which had been established in 1871. In it the president was expected to reign, but not rule. By the time of Australia's federation, all six presidents had behaved politically in office to a greater or lesser degree. Four were forced to resign. There had been a serious possibility of a *coup d'état* by Boulanger. As for politicians choosing the best candidate, the great First World War leader Georges Clemenceau said that he always voted for the most stupid candidate. Sir Henry Maine, the noted nineteenth-century jurist, wrote: "The less we say (of the French president) the better; he is pompous, expensive and perfectly useless." The founders wanted to have nothing to do with a Westminster republic, or even an elected governor-general.

Alfred Deakin, our great founder, said when it was proposed the governor-general be elected:

... the office of governor-general is not one to which a democrat will aspire. To make it an object of ambition you must change its character altogether, and make it an office like that of the President of the United States – a high executive office ...

We are satisfied with all the other offices in the State being open to us, it being possible for the meanest, humblest, and poorest to aspire to the highest office in the commonwealth – that is, the premiership. (Official Report, National Australasian Convention Debates, 2 March to 9 April 1891, pp 570–71)

Sir John Downer added to Alfred Deakin's words. He warned that if the governor-generalship became elective, then he would have a mandate, and a position on all sorts of matters. He would become a competitor to the prime minister.

... I would ask him in what position will the governor-general be when he is elected? If he is elected by the voice of the people, does the Hon. gentleman assume that history will not repeat itself, and that the governor-general will not assume a position something like that of the President of the United States ...

... if we want to retain the authority in the people – apart from the question of whether it is to be in the Senate or the House of Representatives or both coordinately – subject to the authority of the sovereign, it would be inviting at once an inference with that authority to put at the head of the government a person elected by the people, and who, from the very nature of his election, would speak with authority, and assume a dominion over the Commonwealth, which we are certainly not prepared to concede. (Official Report, National Australasian Convention Debates, 2 March to 9 April 1891, pp 571–72)

Sir Samuel Griffith, one of the most eminent of our founders, argued elsewhere in the debates that election of the governor-general either directly or indirectly would not be conducive to the system of government as a whole.

I believe the highest offices of the State ought to be open to its own citizens; but I do not think it follows that the necessary way to bring about that result is to provide that the governor-general shall be directly elected by the people. Probably the greatest difficulties which have arisen in the Untied States are owing to the manner in which the president is there elected. If you have a direct election of the president by the people, or such an indirect election as has been substituted for it there, the practical result would be that at every election for the governor-general there would be a canvassing throughout the whole dominion or commonwealth by the representatives of respective parties, and the governor-general, when elected, would regard himself as the nominee or head of a party, and would devote a great part of his time and attention to securing his re-election . . .

Sir Samuel then made a remarkable prophecy as to how the office of governor-general would develop:

I am much inclined to think that before my years are over not only the governor-general, but the governors of the different Australian colonies, will practically be appointed, not, perhaps, by the direct election, but with the full consent and concurrence, known in advance, of the people of these colonies . . . I have no doubt, especially considering the greatly altered conditions of the Commonwealth, that great weight will be paid to the wishes of the people, and that some means will be found of nominations being made, if not directly by the Australian Commonwealth, yet under such circumstances as to secure appointments which would be known to meet with the concurrence of the people of these colonies. I am of that opinion; I cannot say how it will work out in detail. I believe, also, that when the people of Australia are of opinion – and surely an opinion may be shown in other ways than by an act of parliament – that it is desirable that a distinguished Australian should be appointed to the office of governor-general, some instances will be found – if, indeed, the course is not invariably adopted – in which distinguished Australians will be appointed to the position. That I take it, is all the [one] desires to attain; and it can, compatibly with the retention of our relations with the crown, be attained by leaving the appointment as it is proposed to be left, in the hands of the Queen. (Official Report, National Australasian Convention Debates, 2 March to 9 April 1891, pp 566–67)

WHO WROTE THE AUSTRALIAN CONSTITUTION?

A theme of the recent republican debate has been the allegation that the Australian constitution is not of domestic origin, but rather is the dated work of our imperial overlords. Prime Minister Paul Keating expressed such sentiments on at least two occasions, saying of the constitution in 1993: "It was framed as a routine piece of nineteenth-century British imperial legislation. It shows its age." (*Australian*, 2 August 1993) In 1994 he declared: "Learning about the Constitution apprises people of the fact that we've got a constitution which was designed by the British Foreign Office to look over the Australian Government's shoulder." (*Australian*, 16 June 1994)

True, the present constitution is encased in an imperial statute, but it was essentially the work of local draftsmen, presented to the queen for enactment by the parliament at Westminster only after having first been ratified by the people of each colony at a plebiscite. The imperial parliament had the power to alter the constitution substantially during its passage through the two houses. Nevertheless, the only alteration actually made of any import concerned appeals to the privy council, which have since been abolished. Indeed John Quick and Robert Garran attribute Federation and the constitution under which it was achieved to the efforts of the local communities rather than any colonial masters:

Never before have a group of self-governing, practically independent communities, without external pressure or foreign complications of any kind, deliberately chosen of their own free will to put aside their provincial jealousies and come together as one people, from a simple intellectual and sentimental conviction of the folly of disunion and the advantages of nationhood. The States of America, or Switzerland, or Germany, were drawn together under the shadow of war. Even the Canadian provinces were forced to unite by the neighbourhood of a great foreign power. But the Australian Commonwealth, the fifth great Federation of the world, came into voluntary being through a deep conviction of national unity. We may well be proud of the statesmen who constructed a Constitution which – whatever may be its faults and its shortcomings – has proved acceptable to a large majority of the people of five great communities scattered over a continent; and proud of a people who, without the compulsion of war or the fear of conquest, have succeeded in agreeing upon the terms of a binding and indissoluble Social Compact.

There was no doubt at Westminster that Federation was brought about by Australians. In his second reading speech before the imperial parliament the Earl of Selborne explained:

The Constitution of the United States of America was born of a struggle for colonial independence. The Constitution of the Dominion of Canada was accepted as the solution of internal political troubles constantly recurring over a period of many years ... The consolidation of the German Empire was rendered possible by the victories of a great war. It has remained for the people and the statesmen of Australia alone to determine to federate out of what I may call pure reason. They and they alone, have looked to the future and, as custodians of the interest of their descendants, have determined to consolidate the colonies of Australia in one great Commonwealth. ("Hansard", House of Lords, 29 June 1900)

It cannot be disputed that it was the Australian people and their statesmen that brought about federation.

Clearly then the Colonial Office (let alone the Foreign Office which dealt with non-colonial governments) had no interest in supervising self-government in Australia. Nor did it consciously hinder the ability of local draftsmen in preparing their own constitution.

In any event, the question now is whether Australians are prepared to accept the constitution for what it is – a constituting instrument establishing the organs of a new government and dividing up power between the central government and the municipal governments which together form the federation. Or do they want something more, such as the US *Declaration of Independence*. Is it not too late for this? Even in 1901 it would have been inappropriate. Had independence resulted from a war of independence, or at least a struggle, such rhetoric might have been well chosen. Surely it would be ludicrous now.

WHAT MAKES THE CONSTITUTION BINDING?

The high court explained in 1920 (*Engineers' Case: Amalgamated Society of Engineers v Adelaide Steamship Co. Ltd*, 1920, 28 CLR 129 at 142) that while the constitution is a political compact of the whole of the people of Australia, it was made binding law by an act of the imperial parliament.

This conclusion reflected the fact that in 1900 the formal legality of the constitution and the political causes of federation were seen as logically distinct issues.

But in 1985, Governor-General Sir William Deane, then a Justice of the High Court, questioned the appropriateness of this explanation of the binding character of the constitution:

The authority of the provisions of the Australian *Constitution* and the *Statute of Westminster* rests, as a matter of legal theory, wholly upon their enactment by the Imperial Parliament as distinct from resting upon a wider foundation which also encompasses the social compact and the international agreements which the Constitution and the Statute respectively embodied ... it may, however, be necessary at some future time to consider whether traditional legal theory can properly be regarded as providing an adequate explanation of the process which culminated in the acquisition by Australia of full "independence and sovereignty". (*Kirmani v Captain Cook Cruises*, 1985, 59 ALJR, at 302–303)

A leading constitution lawyer G.J. Lindell observes that while this historical explanation is constitutionally and legally sound, its reliance on Australia's colonial past could lead to a search for an additional, although not necessarily alternative, way of explaining the legally binding character of the constitution. That explanation he said can be found in the words of the preamble, the constitution alteration under section 128 of the constitution, as well as the acquiescence in the continued operation of the constitution as a fundamental law. So the constitution enjoys its character as a higher law because of the will and authority of the people. Such an explanation, he says, more closely conforms to the present social and political reality. It has the advantage of "ensuring that the legal explanation for the binding character of the Constitution coincides with popular understanding". (Lindell 37)

And notwithstanding his view in 1985, Sir William Deane, almost one decade later, had moved on:

The present legitimacy of the Constitution as the compact and highest law of our nation lies exclusively in the original adoption (by referenda) and subsequent maintenance (by acquiescence) of its provisions by the people. (*Theophanous vs Herald & Weekly Times Ltd*, 1994, 182 CLR, 104 at 171)

Politically reality and legal theory are merging. There is a growing acceptance of the proposition that the constitution is a legally binding document because it emanates from the will of the people.

The constitution owes its origin, and continuing life, to the people. Only the people can change it. And when they reject a proposed change, they indicate their continued acceptance of the system. They have demonstrated since federation considerable wisdom in their decisions about change.

EMERGENCE OF NATIONHOOD AND CONSTITUTIONAL CONVENTIONS

An understanding of the gradual development of the role of the crown, including governor-general and the queen, requires such developments to be viewed in the context of the development of Australia as an independent nation. The developments involved changes in convention and, less often, statute. By convention, we mean those usages or customs that are not to be found in the statute books but nevertheless are binding. In jurisdictions governed by a written constitution there is a greater reluctance to acknowledge the role played by convention than there is where no such document exists, as in the United Kingdom.

At the moment our principle concern is directed to the conventions governing the relations between the governments of what were formerly referred to as dominions, now realms, and that of the United Kingdom and those governing the role of the governor-general.

The federal constitution is concerned primarily with the division and separation of powers within Australia. It is not expressly concerned with resolving questions of nationhood or independence. A survey of Australian constitutional history reveals that Australia acquired independence by a gradual process – although the late Justice Lionel Murphy held that because Australians could change our constitution, we became independent in 1901. (*China Ocean Shipping Co. v South Australia,* 1978–1979, 145, CLR at 236, 237, 239)

A gauge by which independence may be measured is the willingness of foreign national governments to enter into treaties with Australia. Justice Barry O'Keefe reminds us that after the First World War Australia was represented independently at the peace negotiations by Prime Minister Billy Hughes. He presses the argument that Australia was a self-governing country, not subordinate to the parliament at Westminster, but rather a partner with equality of status, not necessarily (at that time) equality of stature. That argument was accepted as a hard practical fact by the nations, including Britain, that took part in the peace negotiations. Independence was well established in the international scene by 1920.

Australian independence came to be recognised at the Imperial Conferences of Dominion and British prime ministers convened in 1917, 1926 and 1930. According to the *Balfour Declaration*, the dominions were autonomous communities within the British Empire, equal in status, in no way subordinate one to another in any aspect of their domestic or external affairs, though united by a common allegiance to the crown, and freely associated, as members of the British Commonwealth of Nations.

This result was explained at the 1992 conference in these words:

The rapid evolution of the overseas dominions during the last fifty years has involved many complicated adjustments of old political machinery to changing conditions. The tendency towards equality of status was both right *and* inevitable. Geographical and other conditions made this impossible of attainment by the way of federation. The only alternative was by the way of autonomy; and along this road it has been steadily sought. Every self-governing member of the Empire is now the master of its destiny. In fact, if not always in form, it is subject to no compulsion whatever.

The *Balfour Declaration* recognised conventions that had already developed. The *Declaration* was given statutory effect when the parliament at Westminster passed the *Statute of Westminster*, 1931, which recognised the full emancipation of the dominion parliaments. Now they could enact laws repugnant to the law of England (section 2), and give "extraterritorial" effect to any legislation (section 3). The statute limits the competence of the United Kingdom to legislate for the dominions to circumstances in which the relevant parliament requested and consented to such imperial legislation (section 4). The act stipulated that the operation of the dominion constitution was not affected in any way (section 7 and section 8). It also stipulated that unlike the Canadian provinces to which it would apply, the act would not apply to the Australian states. This was at their request (section 9). Finally, the act would not have any effect in Australia until the parliament of the Commonwealth of Australia adopted the act itself by means of an adopting act (s10). In fact the commonwealth parliament did not adopt the statute until 1942, at which time the act was given a retrospective operation "as from the commencement of the war between His Majesty the King and Germany".

The precise point at which independence was attained remains a moot point. Was it the political compact? Was it the formal offer by the mother parliament? Or was it the formal acceptance of the offer by the newly independent dominion parliament? In a fairly recent judgement, Lord Denning MR maintains independence came as a matter of evolving usage and convention rather than by means of enactment:

Hitherto I have said that in constitutional law the crown was single and indivisible. But that law was changed in the first half of this century – not by statute – but by constitutional usage and practice. (*R vs Secretary of State for Foreign and Commonwealth Affairs ex parte Indian Association of Alberta*, 1982, 2 WLR, 641, at 651)

The passage highlights the role conventions have played in the evolving relationship between governments within the British Empire and the subsequent Commonwealth of Nations. Were such relations governed by the rigidity of statute such developments could not occur so naturally as need requires. The gradual emergence of full Australian nationhood was possible precisely because of the flexibility that is offered by convention.

It has been argued that legal independence did not occur until the passage of the *Statute of Westminster* through both imperial and dominion parliaments was complete. In a passage dealing with the difficulty of making such a determination, Chief Justice Sir Garfield Barwick said:

The historical movement of Australia to the status of a fully independent nation has been both gradual and, to a degree, imperceptible ... though the precise day of the acquisition of national independence may not be identifiable, it certainly was not the date of the inauguration of the Commonwealth in 1901. The historical, political and legal reality is that from 1901 until some period of time subsequent to the passage and adoption of the *Statute of Westminster*, the Commonwealth was no more than a self-governing colony though latterly having dominion status. (*China Ocean Shipping Co. v South Australia*, 1979, 145, CLR 172 at 183)

The position was certainly resolved by the *Australia Acts* of 1986, which make certain that Australia is absolutely independent of the United Kingdom. Sir Anthony Mason, then Chief Justice of

Australia, held this to be the true date of a hand-over of sovereignty, explaining that the *Australia Acts*: "marked the end of the legal sovereignty of the imperial parliament and recognised that ultimate sovereignty resided in the Australian people". (*Australian Capital Television Ltd v Commonwealth*, 1992, 177, CLR 106 at 138)

With the *Balfour Declaration* and the *Statute of Westminster* had come the termination of British legislative and executive responsibility, at least for the commonwealth, if not the states. Judicial responsibility remained, however, until the termination of appeals to the privy council (Her Majesty in Council), which had become part of the Australian court structure.

There are four significant points about the *Australia Acts*, 1986. Firstly, the bulk of the acts is concerned with severing those remaining legal ties between the states and the United Kingdom. These gave the state legislatures the full powers that the United Kingdom had previously retained – at Australia's request – to legislate for the state as well as the power to legislate extra-territorially. The *Colonial Laws Validity Act*, 1865, and the doctrine prohibiting repugnance to the law of England no longer applied (section 6). British executive responsibility and privy council appeals from the state disappeared (section 10 and section 11).

Secondly, the *Acts* clarify the role of the queen and the governors in respect of the states. The state premiers would give advice on the exercise of royal powers, not through the British government, but direct to the queen. The premiers were never prepared to go through Canberra.

Thirdly, the *Statute of Westminster* was amended in several respects. These included the termination of the power of the United Kingdom parliament to legislate for the commonwealth, the states and territories thereof, even at the request of the Australian parliaments. (Notwithstanding this, over recent years some republicans have made the bizarre suggestion that the British parliament should be requested to impose a republic!) Now no British Act can henceforth apply to any Australian jurisdiction (section 11 and section 12).

Fourth, the *Acts* stipulate that the *Commonwealth of Australia Constitution Act* and the *Statute of Westminster* continue to be in force, and provide an intricate method by which the *Australia Acts* and the *Statute of Westminster* may be amended.

Both *Acts*, enacted in substantially identical terms by the United Kingdom and Australian parliaments, were proclaimed by the queen to come into effect on 3 March 1986. On arrival in Australia to proclaim the Australian version, she observed both the rise of an Australian national identity and the circumstances under which the constitutional relationship between Australia and the United Kingdom had come to an end:

I can see a growing sense of identity and a fierce pride in being Australian. So it is right that the *Australia Acts* has finally severed the last of the Constitutional links between Australia and Britain, and I was glad to play a dual role in this. My last official action as Queen of the United Kingdom before leaving London last month was to give my assent to the *Australia Acts* from the Westminster Parliament. My first official action on arriving in Australia yesterday was to proclaim an identical Act – but from the Australia Parliament – which I did as Queen of Australia. Surely no two independent countries could bring to an end their constitutional relationship in a more civilised way, and I hope you will agree with me that this has been symbolic of the depth and quality of the relationship between Australia and Britain. Anachronistic constitutional arrangements have disappeared – but the friendship between two nations has been strengthened and will endure. (McDonald, 67)

What we have seen since the adoption of the Australian constitution is the gradual emergence of Australia as an independent nation. This surely is one of the beauties of our system – that it has permitted such a peaceful evolution.

As Sir Harry Gibbs explains:

Our Constitution has been criticised because it sketches the outline of the system of government and does not set out in detail the rules and conventions that determine the working of the various arms of government. Any such criticism is totally misconceived. The strength of our Constitution, as it has been the strength of the Constitution of the United Kingdom, is that it allows the needs of a changing society to be met by a gradual development, which has been found impossible in some nations whose written Constitutions attempt to lay down all the rules in detail. (Gibbs, 1994)

THE DEVELOPING ROLE OF THE QUEEN AND THE GOVERNOR-GENERAL IN THE CONSTITUTION

Our task now is to plot the constitutional development of the office of governor-general, and that of the sovereign. Here we shall not presently be concerned with issues such as the reserve powers other than to the extent that they affect the development of these offices. The role of both governor-general and sovereign has evolved to meet changing needs as Australia emerged as an independent and self-determining nation.

How did the founders of our constitution view the role of the governor-general? In their commentary on the constitution, Quick and Garran discuss the role of a colonial governor. They quote from Merivale's "Lecture on Colonisation", 1861, where it is explained that a vice-regal representative has a dual role: "He has to reconcile, as well as he can, his double function as governor representing the crown, and as a constitutional head of an executive." (Quick and Garran 388) The reference to the crown here is of course to the imperial crown, that is the British government.

Even in 1861 the vice-regal representative was understood to be principally the constitutional umpire and auditor. This becomes significant in the contemporary disputes about who is in fact the head of state. As far back as 1873, Lord Dufferin, when governor-general of Canada, understood himself to be: "The head of a constitutional state, engaged in the administration of parliamentary government."

The dual role was changed in 1926 by the adoption of the *Report of the Inter-Imperial Relations Committee* to the Imperial Conference.

This referred to the previous practice of appointments being made solely on the advice of His Majesty's ministers in London. The Report stated:

In our opinion it is an essential consequence of the equality of status existing among the member of the British Commonwealth of Nations that the governor-general of a dominion is the representative of the crown, holding in all essential respects the same position in relation to the administration of public affairs in the dominion as is held by His Majesty the King in Great Britain, and that he is not the representative or agent of His Majesty's Government in Great Britain or of any Department of that Government.

It seemed to us to follow that the practice whereby the governor-general of a dominion is the formal official channel of communication between His Majesty's Government in Great Britain and His Governments in the dominions might be regarded as no longer wholly in accordance with the constitutional position of the governor-general. It was thought that the recognised official channel of communication should be, in future, between government and government direct . . . it was recognised by the Committee, as an essential feature of any change or development in the channels of communication, that a governor-general should be supplied with copies of all documents of importance and in general should be kept as fully informed as is His Majesty the King in Great Britain of Cabinet business and public affairs.

Thus the conference affirmed the abolition of the governor-general's residual role as representative of the British government in Australia, but in doing so it did not declare him head of the executive or head of state. Why? For this he already was. The emphasis on the idea that the governor-general should stand in the same relation to the dominion government as that in which the King stood to the British government clearly indicates this. As the dominions increased their already substantial exterior roles, the governor-general became accepted internationally as a head of state, that rarefied term hitherto used only by diplomats and international lawyers.

Although the method of appointing the governor-general could no longer involve the British government, the new process was not clarified until the conference of 1930, at which the following six principles were confirmed:

The parties interested in the appointment of a governor-general of a dominion are His Majesty the King, whose representative he is, and the dominion concerned.

The constitutional practice that His Majesty acts on the advice of responsible ministers applies also in this instance.

The ministers who tender advice and are responsible for such advice are His Majesty's ministers in the dominion concerned.

The ministers concerned tender their formal advice after informal consultation with His Majesty. (This surely puts paid to the false proposition that the Queen might instantly remove a governor-general on a phone call from the prime minister, and makes more glaring the awesome power of instant dismissal the prime minister would have under a Keating–Turnbull republic.)

The channel of communication between His Majesty and the government of any dominion is a matter solely concerning His Majesty and such government.

The manner in which the instrument containing the governor-general's appointment should reflect the principles set forth above is a matter in regard to which His Majesty is advised by his ministers in the dominion concerned.

Sir David Smith says that the conference decision was taken at the height of, and in support of, action initiated earlier that year by Australia's Prime Minister J.H. Scullin who insisted on advising the King on the appointment of an Australian as governor-general. "Scullin's insistence on the right to recommend the appointment of Sir Isaac Isaacs as Australia's first Australian-born governor-general became the genesis of the new rule for the appointment of governors-general throughout the Empire." (Smith, 1997, 5–6) The king had argued, unsuccessfully, that there was an advantage for Australia in having someone who had not played a political or other role in Australia.

The 1926 and the 1930 Imperial Conference decisions changed the status of the vice-regal office and established a new relationship between the governor-general and the Australian government. "What we did was alter our constitutional arrangements to meet evolving constitutional needs, but without having to alter one word of the constitution itself. These changes are perfect examples of the far-sightedness of our founders, and evidence of the adaptability and flexibility of our allegedly horse-and-buggy and inflexible Constitution." (Smith, 1997, 5–6)

Although Sir Isaac Isaacs was succeeded by a number of British appointments, since the appointment of Lord Casey (himself formerly a governor of Bengal in 1965) the office has been consistently filled by Australian residents. It was argued by some in Australia in the 1950s that appointments should be made from other commonwealth countries. There was a vague proposal, for instance, that Mrs Pandit, sister of the Indian prime minister, should be made governor-general.

So we have in the governor-general, a head of the executive and head of a constitutional state who stands in the same relation to the Australian government as the queen does to the United Kingdom's, who is appointed on the advice of Her Majesty's Australian ministers and who is normally an Australian citizen with appropriate qualifications. There is no legal restriction on a person who has dual citizenship becoming governor-general, unlike members of the federal parliament.

What is the status of the queen according to Australian constitutional law? Perhaps the greatest development on this front has been the recognition of the divisibility of the crown, confirmed by the high court in *Sue vs Hill*, 23 June 1999. To understand this requires us to return once more to the Imperial Conference of

1926. Prior to this time, the crown had been regarded as indivisible, the majority in the *Engineers'* case in 1920, for instance, explaining:

The crown . . . is one and indivisible throughout the Empire . . . The first step in the examination of the Constitution is to emphasise the primary legal axiom that the crown is ubiquitous and indivisible in the king's dominions.

As we have seen, the *Balfour Declaration* took the crown in a new direction. It provided the beginnings of a new theory wherein there could be one common monarch who wore multiple crowns, each of which represents a logically distinct legal person. The preamble to the *Statute of Westminster* 1931 states:

. . . in as much as the crown is the symbol to the free association of the members of the British Commonwealth of Nations, and as they are united by a common allegiance to the crown, it would be in accord with the established constitutional position of all the members of the Commonwealth in relation to one another that any law touching upon the succession to the Throne or the Royal Style and Titles shall hereafter require the assent of the Parliaments of all the dominions and the Parliament of the United Kingdom.

The proposition about the succession was tested by the abdication crisis of 1936 when the Australian prime minister replied to the British prime minister's telegram asking whether Australia would support a morganatic marriage between Edward VIII and Wallis Simpson, that is, one which would have no constitutional significance or effect:

There would be outspoken hostility to His Majesty's proposed wife becoming Queen, while any proposal that she should become Consort and not Queen . . . would not be approved by my Government. (Ziegler, 305–306)

Subsequently, the *Abdication Act (Imp.)*, 1936, received the assent of the commonwealth parliament by resolution of both houses. The second point in the preamble was dealt with by means of the *Royal Style and Titles Acts*, 1953. In this the commonwealth parliament provided for a unique royal style and title for use in Australia. This followed the commonwealth prime ministers' conference of the previous year at which it was decided that a common style and titles was not needed throughout the commonwealth so long as a common element was retained.

The title agreed to in 1926 had been *George V, by the Grace of God, of the United Kingdom of Great Britain, Ireland and of the British Dominions beyond the Seas King, Defender of the Faith, Emperor of India*. This had been updated in 1947, substituting *Head of the Commonwealth* for *Emperor of India* upon Indian independence.

The new style and titles adopted by the *Royal Style and Titles Act* 1953 (Cth) for exclusive use in Australia was *Elizabeth the Second, by the Grace of God of the United Kingdom, Australia and Her other Realms and Territories Queen, Head of the Commonwealth, Defender of the Faith*. This was altered in 1973 to the present *Royal Style and Titles*, which reads *Elizabeth the Second, by the Grace of God Queen of Australia and Her other Realms and Territories, Head of the Commonwealth*. Queen Elizabeth II said at Parliament House, Canberra on 18 October 1973:

The reality and dynamic quality of the relationship between crown and people will be symbolised in another way tomorrow when I give my Assent in person to an Act of the Australia Parliament which amends my Style and Title. It puts Queen of Australia first and foremost. It will give me much satisfaction to do this because it is realistic, because it is something which my father thought should be done as long ago as 1947 and, above all, because I hope it will strengthen that relationship which I value and cherish.

So the office of the Queen of Australia has evolved into a legally separate and distinct person, as a result of a gentle process commenced at the Imperial Conference of 1926. A majority of the high court in *Nolan vs Minister for Immigration and Ethnic Affairs* (1988) 165 CLR 178 held:

The transition from Empire to Commonwealth and the emergence of Australia and other dominions as independent sovereign nations . . . inevitably changed the nature of the relationship between the United Kingdom and its former colonies and rendered obsolete notions of an indivisible crown . . . It became accepted as a truism that, although there is only one person who is the sovereign . . . in matters of law and government the Queen of the United Kingdom . . . is entirely distinct from the Queen of (eg) Canada or Australia.

Having examined the development of the office of the governor-general and the emergence of the Queen of Australia as a distinct entity, I now make some final comment about the relationship between the two offices.

The *Constitution* clearly hands the queen's power over to the governor-general (ss2 and 61). However this appears to have been largely overlooked both in Britain and Australia, with Queen Victoria issuing *Letters Patent and Instructions* – subsequently revised by Kind Edward VII in 1902, King George V in 1920 and Queen Elizabeth II in 1958. When the error was realised, the queen revoked Queen Victoria's *Letters Patent* and issued new ones on the advice of Prime Minister Hawke in 1984. (Smith, 4, 8)

The reason that the sovereign may in no way interfere in the governor-general's activities stems from section 61 of the constitution which, unlike the state constitutions or that of Canada, stipulates that while the executive power of the commonwealth is vested in the queen, it is exercisable by the governor-general alone. This became apparent to Lord Haldane during argument in the application for special leave to appeal the high court's decision in the *Engineers'* case to the privy council when he asked of section 61: "Does it not put the sovereign in the position of having parted, so far as the affairs of the commonwealth are concerned, with every shadow of active intervention in their affairs and handing them over, unlike the case of Canada, to the governor-general?" (Evatt, 311)

This interpretation was confirmed by the passage of the *Royal Powers Act*, 1953 (Cth). In preparing for the Royal visit of 1954, it became apparent to Prime Minister Menzies that the constitution prohibited the governor-general from delegating any of his powers, which were totally his, even to his sovereign. Thus it is apparent that the vice-regal representative is *no mere representative*. The new act provided that the queen could exercise any of the governor-general's statutory but not constitutional powers while personally present in Australia if so advised by her Australian ministers, though this does not preclude the governor-general from continuing to exercise such powers simultaneously. The argument heard in the privy council and in cabinet was put from Buckingham Palace in 1975 when the speaker of the house of representatives was advised that the queen could not interfere in the constitutional crisis:

As we understand the situation here, the Australian Constitution firmly places the prerogative powers of the crown in the hands of the governor-general as the representative of the Queen of Australia. The only person competent to commission an Australia prime minister is the governor-general, and the Queen has no part in the decisions which the governor-general must take in accordance with the Constitution. Her Majesty, as Queen of Australia, is watching events in Canberra with close interest and attention, but it would not be proper for her to intervene in person in matters which are so clearly placed within the jurisdiction of the governor-general by the Constitution Act. (Kerr, 330)

The true position of the governor-general was summed up by the Constitutional Commission in 1988 which concluded that: "Although the governor-general is the queen's representative in Australia, the governor-general is in no sense a *delegate* of the queen." (para 5.17)

6

THE FIRST
KEATING–TURNBULL REPUBLIC

In his foreword to *The Australian Constitution*, Sir Harry Gibbs writes:

The greatest potential weakness of any democratic constitution is that it may permit a government which has secured a bare majority of votes – or a majority of seats with even a minority of votes – to act as a tyranny and to bring about fundamental changes which may be destructive of democracy itself. Our Constitution contains checks and balances, which render such a situation unlikely if not impossible. The existence of the states, the power of the senate and the fact that the governor-general represents, and may be removed by, the Queen all contribute to place restrictions on the unbridled exercise of political power. Some politicians, who feel frustration that they cannot more easily get their own way, would remove, if they could, some or all of these restraints on power. We should view with suspicion any attempt to weaken the checks and balances in the constitution which has served us so well.

In 1993 Prime Minister Paul Keating established a Republic Advisory Committee (RAC) to advise him on the various options for minimal change necessary to bring about republican government in Australia. The RAC's terms of reference stipulated that it should not address any broader issues regarding other areas of constitutional reform or the normative question of whether Australia ought to become a republic. It should also not make any final recommendations, but rather address the advantages and disadvantages of the possible approaches to a specified list of matters. (RAC, Vol. 1, p iv)

So the Republic Advisory Committee was not intended to debate the advantages or disadvantages of a republic over the existing system. Its formation reflected Keating's adversarial style. He once argued that the first question about a republic was: "Do you support an Australian republic?" Only if you supported such an entity were you to be admitted to the forum that would discuss the form of the republic. This theme was brutally applied both in terms of reference and of the membership – totally republican – of the RAC. It was chaired by Malcolm Turnbull, the leader of the Australian Republican Movement.

When the prime minister gave his response to the report, he endorsed the desirability of Australia becoming a republic on the basis of a "minimal" change to the constitution. He addressed five areas of change. The principle components involved:

- The creation of an office of head of state – a novelty for Australians, most of whom had never heard of this term. It was to be styled 'president' and the qualifications for candidacy stipulating citizenship and age requirements were set out.

- Appointment and dismissal procedures, both to be effected by a two-thirds majority of a joint sitting of the commonwealth parliament, the former on the nomination of a single candidate by the prime minister, the latter on the motion of either house receiving a simple majority. Importantly the committee found an almost universal view that the president should not hold office at the whim of the prime minister.

- A constitutional statement entrenching the continuity of the exercise of the governor-general's powers by the president and the constitutional conventions governing the exercise thereof, with no codification of the reserve powers

- Preservation of the self-determination of constitutional arrangements for the states so that the states could remain constitutional monarchies.

- Consequential alterations to remove monarchical references without altering the practical effect of various provisions.

It was Keating's stated intention that the transition to a republic would be a small step, albeit a highly significant one, with minimal disruption to the system by which Australia is governed. There was dissent in the republican ranks, however, as to just how small the step being proposed was. One democratic republican, the late Professor Patrick O'Brien, explained:

In his speech, Keating repeated the false claim that the move from a constitutional monarchy to a republic was a small step. It is a giant leap. Of itself, the institution of a republic means the institution of a new constitution and a new political order. Whether it is a giant leap forward or backwards, therefore, depends upon the constitutional distribution, weighing and checking and balancing of power and authority among the people, the parliament, the executive, the bureaucracy and the High Court. (O'Brien, 158)

It was quite clear that Professor O'Brien saw the Keating–Turnbull model as a giant leap backwards.

APPOINTING THE PRESIDENT

The first Keating–Turnbull model has met with both practical and ideological criticism. Despite strong electoral support for popular election, the Keating government advocated parliamentary appointment and dismissal. Clerk of the Senate Harry Evans has argued against this method of appointment on principle:

Most people, not being intellectuals, are able to detect the massive contradiction at the heart of the elite orthodoxy: the monarchy must go partly because it is undemocratic, but the people must not be allowed to choose the replacement, because they would stupidly make the wrong choice. (*News Weekly,* 29 July 1997)

Bill Hayden, a former governor-general, warns of the practical effect of election by special parliamentary majority:

Those who believe a president elected by both Houses of Parliament would attract nominations from the 'best people in the community', need to be reminded of the adversarial structure of our political system. The hectoring style of so many Senate Committee hearings is illustrative of the sort of grinding and very personal inquisition to which a nominee could be subjected. The process here would make the Supreme Court confirmation hearings of the USA Senate, such as in the cases of Dinks and Hill, look like a suburban manse morning tea party. The prospect of such an experience would discourage all but the stout-hearted. (Hayden, 548–549)

The election of the president would be by a joint sitting of both houses of the federal parliament. So the greatest say would be to the most populous states, effectively the Canberra, Sydney, Melbourne axis. A two-thirds majority would be required.

It would be a strange election, at least outside of the totalitarian countries. There would only be one candidate, just as in the old Soviet Union. The thinking was that at least the government and opposition would have had to support the candidate. This is not guaranteed. The Fraser government came close to having a two-thirds majority. A change by legislation of the method of election of the senate could easily increase the likelihood of governments commanding this majority. This does not need a constitutional amendment. It can be done by legislation.

In the meantime the attempt to force an agreement on government and opposition assumes that both will act in the best interests of the nation to choose the best candidate. What will obviously happen will be a deal. In return for support for a candidate, the other side will agree to support some measure or not take some action – secretly of course.

Australians have already seen, and are disenchanted by this wheeling and dealing.

The American founders saw the danger of deals between politicians and with the candidate, both on election and re-election. So they decided to remove the politicians from the electoral process for the president.

And even a single candidate election is still an election. As minister Bronwyn Bishop says, in an election the candidate has to stand for something – his or her platform. By winning he or she has a mandate. This is totally unlike the non-political governor-general who has neither a platform not a mandate. So what do we have under this republic? A politician chosen by politicians. And with an enormous mandate – two-thirds of parliament. The prime minister, by contrast, may have a little over half the house and a minority in senate. Who would have the biggest mandate?

DISMISSING THE PRESIDENT

Perhaps the most serious problem with the first Keating–Turnbull republic was that raised by one with first-hand experience of vice-regal office, Richard McGarvie, who warns against the threat to democracy that would result from instituting a head of state who was not readily dismissible:

The fatal flaw of the models many republicans still support is that a president elected by parliament or the people could not be promptly dismissed. That sanction for breach, which gives binding effect to the convention of exercising the great powers of head of state as elected ministers advise, would disappear. Oppositions do not support governments. No federal government for fifty years has had that majority. Even if it did, a president could stymie dismissal by exercising the power to dissolve or adjourn (prorogue) parliament. Our democracy depends on the sanction of dismissal and if it evaporates so will democracy. (*Adelaide Review*, December 1997)

My view at the time was that without codification, this proposal would import into Australia something like the French Fifth Republic, where a powerful president "cohabits" uneasily with a parliamentary prime minister. The French have such a system only because their efforts to have a US-style republic, or the Westminster system failed. The ARM's reaction to this and other ACM criticisms was to denounce our arguments as scare-mongering.

CODIFICATION OF THE RESERVE POWERS

The basis of the new presidency under the Keating government's model was that the new head of state would simply "slip in" to the role presently carried out by the governor-general. Republican Professor Patrick O'Brien argues that the governor-generalship cannot be stripped of its monarchical overtones:

Abolish the crown and you thereby also abolish the office of governor-general. Its political and metaphysical functions cannot simply be transferred to another office, regardless of what it is called. These powers are inseparable from the crown. The fashioners of the United States Constitution understood this simple point. Hence the creation of the brand new executive offices ... following two decades of the most intense, polemical debate about the future constitutional shape of their proposed republic. (O'Brien, 159–160)

The staunchest of republicans and the staunchest of monarchists find themselves bedfellows in their common opposition to the Keating government's attempt to graft a republican institution on to our monarchical constitution. As Professor Lane observed, rather than attempting to graft a republic on to a monarchical constitution, republicans should develop a new constitution. Justice Lloyd Waddy, as Convenor of ACM, wrote that the way to achieve a republic is a radical rewrite of the constitution as the Americans did, not merely preserving the present arrangements but severing them from their source of legitimacy:

When I begin most speeches on republicanism, I make two basic statements. First, I say, Of course, we can have republic if a sufficient majority vote for it. If the Americans can run a republic for two hundred years with only one (very bloody) civil war, Australians could run two republics before breakfast. Secondly, I add, If you want me to nominate a republican system I would presently favour, it is that of the USA; we know it is safe and that it works, in its way, and has done so for over two hundred years. But I must confess that I believe the operation of its system of government, with an executive-style presidency is infinitely inferior to our own. (Grainger and Jones, 101)

One of the greatest sticking points of Prime Minister Keating's speech responding to the RAC's report, however, was his preferred treatment of the reserve powers of the crown – the powers which do not require the advice of the ministers of the crown. Under the first Keating–Turnbull republic, the reserve powers of the governor-general would continue to be exercisable by the president but they would remain uncodified. Rather, a provision would be inserted into the constitution providing that the informal conventions governing the operation of the vice-regal reserve powers – whatever they may be – would continue to operate to bind the new head of state.

The failure to codify the circumstances in which the reserve powers could be exercised was deemed catastrophic by some republicans. Writer Donald Horne explained shortly after the Keating proposal was announced that:

Since a president would be harder to get rid of than a governor-general, it is prudent for us to change our Constitution to say what powers a president has, and therefore, by inference, what powers a president does not have … after a referendum, we would insert into the Constitution a section saying that, except in specified circumstances, the president would act only on the advice of the government. (*Sydney Morning Herald*, 27 October 1995)

He said that: "Without a clear statement of the president's powers even I will vote No in a referendum." (*Sydney Morning Herald*, 3 June 1995)

Malcolm Turnbull similarly favoured codification although he supported Keating's method of appointment. He has emphatically declared that: "I support full codification of the powers of the president." (Turnbull, 166)

The ARM Platform adopted a similar stance: "The functions of the president shall be spelt out in the Constitution."

There appear to have been two grounds for arguing against codification. One revolves around the difficulty of the exercise. As Senator Gareth Evans explained, the "definition [of the present controversial unwritten conventions would be] a labour of Hercules. Reformers would have to devote thirty years to the task to have an impact ... Frankly, I think the task is impossible." (*Australian Financial Review*, 9 May, 1995) In other words, the problem about codification already exists in the present arrangements and concentration on the problem will only hinder progress towards a republic.

Professor O'Brien argues that however desirable and effective non-codification has been, it is a creature of historical developments that will necessarily disappear.

The removal of the crown, he says, "will also mean the removal of these royal prerogatives and reserve powers, whatever they are". He asks in whose name will the powers be exercised – the prime minister's, the parliament's, the high court's, or the people's? What will be the source of those powers? How are they to be defined and in relation to what? What will be the due processes governing the office and its relationship with other major institutions of government? Surely, he writes, these and numerous other questions must be answered to the satisfaction of the people and be codified. And if these powers are not conferred upon the president by a majority of the people at a free election, the president would be deprived of the respect of the people. The incumbent will correctly be perceived as parliament's and the executive's poodle.

It appears that the proponents of this republic have thrown up their hands in despair. They say that codifying the reserve powers is far too difficult. But if Australia is to become a republic, surely you have to set out the powers of each of the offices of the republic. The crown has been removed and these conventions depended for their life on the crown. Some might say that it is more a matter of luck than design that Australia's constitutional arrangements are as they are. But is that not the very advantage of evolution over revolution? Were it not for particular historical developments we might not now have the flexible arrangements presently enjoyed. A republic will and must change the existing structures. This was played down by the Keating government to make the product appear more marketable. Yet without the crown, we have an inherently unstable mixture.

On the one side we have those, such as Dr John Hirst the historian who still wants the flexibility of uncodified powers to be carried into the Keating–Turnbull republic. On the other side are Horne and O'Brien and the warning that codification is necessary if a new institution is to be established. The crisis is between the desirability of flexible arrangements and the knowledge that a new order must provide all its own rules, not rely on the conventions of the one it supersedes. It is clear that republicans cannot have it both ways.

The Keating–Turnbull model expects that the new president would represent Australia overseas and be the embodiment of Australian identity.

High Court Justice Michael Kirby, for instance, rejects the suggestion that the president should of necessity, represent the nation's interests overseas in a way the queen does:

To the complaint that the Queen is not, when overseas, seen as a representative of Australia, a ready answer may be given: the Prime Minister should be the main representative of Australia overseas. We can survive the shame of a nineteen-gun salute. Our system is Parliamentary. That means a Prime Minister. Let him or her be Australia's representative overseas. And in the unlikely event that the people of Asia, or anywhere else, care the slightest about our constitutional arrangements, let them mind their own business. Just as we mind ours in relation to their constitutions. Such things are the product of history and sentiment and are not always susceptible to easy explication to neighbours.

And when it is lamented that the queen never represents us overseas as Queen of Australia, a further answer is obvious. Her Australian ministers have never advised her to do this. In fact, the governor-general has occasionally represented us, but more frequently it has been the role of the prime minister and the ministers.

The other key role of Keating's president is to be the embodiment of the Australian national identity. Chancellor of the University of Sydney Dame Leonie Kramer explained in a speech at the ACM launch on 4 June 1993 that there can be no one exhaustive expression of such an identity:

As for the question of identity, suffice it to say that there is no reason why individual Australians should subscribe to some common notion of what it is to be Australian. There is room for all the differences of opinion that a mixed society such as ours can contain . . . what does matter is that we share common values relating to democratic policies and practices, representative government, a non-political legal system, private enterprise, educational systems committed to high standards in teaching and learning, equality of opportunity, and tolerance of others' views – in short, a free society. The best guarantee of the maintenance of these values is our indigenous form of constitutional monarchy.

In fact, to most Australians the national identity is about respect for democracy, the rule of law, tolerance, English as the national language and freedom of expression. For the small elite, a new presidency may seem to be a strong assertion of Australian identity and independence. But this is not at all true of the rank and file. As Geoffrey Horne said at the 1998 Constitutional Convention:

Becoming more competitive in trade with our Asian neighbours . . . would assert our freedom and independence more. Having the Wallabies beat the All Blacks or the Socceroos reach the World Cup finals would more effectively assert our independence as a nation, and fixing unemployment and domestic matters would have more effect in asserting ourselves as free people in an independent nation. (*Report of the Constitutional Convention*, 2–13 February 1998, Vol III)

THE STATES

Our final problem before leaving the first Keating–Turnbull republic, is its treatment of the states. The states were to be involved in two ways. The first is that each state forms its own constitutional monarchy distinct from each other and the commonwealth. If only the part of the constitutional monarchy at the federal level is abolished, the question arises as to whether this would have any impact on the continuity of the six state monarchies. If not, ought the states be forced to change their constitutional arrangements? Secondly, the question arises as to what role, if any, the states might have to play in the changes required to bring about a republic at the federal level even if no change were to occur at the state level.

It was the view of the prime minister that there would be no necessary implications for the states were the commonwealth alone to become a republic, and the government had no intention of exerting any pressure on the states to make their arrangements consonant with those of a new republican commonwealth:

It is not our intention that the government's proposals should affect the Constitutions of the Australian states. It would be up to each state to decide how in future they would appoint their respective heads of state. It is reasonable to expect that if the Australian people opt for an Australian head of state, the states would follow suit. But the question would be for each state to decide.

In this way the difficulty of forcing the states to change was avoided and an ordinary section 128 referendum would be sufficient to establish a federal republic requiring a national majority and a majority in only four rather than all six states. However there are good arguments that, this being a fundamental issue, the consent of the six states is necessary.

Should such a referendum be carried with only four states' support, it is conceivable that the legislation might be contested by one of the other two states on the basis that there is only one crown in Australia (albeit with seven manifestations). The destruction of that crown, it might be argued, would go to the heart of the original compact, thus constituting a renegotiation of the terms of the initial "indissoluble" compact to establish an indissoluble federal commonwealth under the crown. Furthermore, if the crown is one with various manifestations rather than seven separate crowns, destruction of it might constitute an action by the commonwealth disabling a state to operate in a fundamental sense.

Support for such a conception of the crown is to be found in Justice Rich's approach in *Minister for Works (WA) vs Gulson* (1944), 69 CLR 338 at 356 where he explains:

It is by the crown that all legislative and administrative authority is exercised throughout the Empire, although in each constitutional area such authority can be exercised by the crown only through the agencies of the appropriate Parliament and the appropriate group of constitutional ministers, so that legalistically, it would be more strictly accurate to speak of the state of Western Australia in right of the crown than of the crown in right of the state of Western Australia.

It is clear that the single indivisible imperial crown under which Australia federated had become several crowns, but only down to an Australian, or a Canadian, or a New Zealand crown. The crown in Australia is one and indivisible. If it were the seven crowns that the RAC suggests, the indissoluble federal commonwealth established in 1901 would be effectively dissolved. Each state could go its own way. A devastating result, unless you tried to overcome this by constitutional amendments dividing the Australian crown seven ways and abolishing one of them.

These questions could require further determination by the high court, and the first Keating–Turnbull republic was criticised by both monarchists and republicans on these grounds. For five years, the ARM insisted on the rectitude of this model. They scoffed at any criticism.

And then, in the last days of the Constitutional Convention, without any adequate explanation, they changed the model to prove that the Australian president, unlike any other in the world, would hold office at the whim of the prime minister.

7
THE CONVENTION

In the summer of 1998, Robert Manne, Associate Professor in Politics at Monash University and a regular columnist, wrote with some surprise in the *Sydney Morning Herald* (1 February 1999) about what he described as the "infighting" between Australia's republicans. Even if the republican camp were united, he said, the difficulties in the coming referendum of persuading both a majority of Australians and a majority of states would have proved immense. But with an "internally divided, self-lacerating republican movement" these difficulties would prove insurmountable. He wrote: "In a way no Australian monarchist at the Constitutional Convention could have predicted, this fatal contradiction at the heart of Australian republicanism had emerged."

But the phenomenon of republicans fighting among themselves is hardly new. The examples of Cromwell's Roundheads against the Levellers, between the French Girondins and the Jacobins, between the Russian Mensheviks and the Bolsheviks, between the Stalinists and the Trotskyists, spring to mind.

In the more refined atmosphere of the 1998 Constitutional Convention, the divisions were no less clear. And notwithstanding Manne's surprise, they were just as predictable.

The words republic, and indeed republicanism, have just too many meanings to be useful.

The call repeated over and over that Australia should hold a plebiscite on whether Australians wish Australia to become a republic, and the endless political and media talk of "the" republic ignore this fundamental point. As do most opinion polls. It is now clear that what the ARM means by republic is a tightly controlled republic, in which the crown does not exist. In other words, get rid of the crown at any price.

Unlike the ARM, real republicans are more interested in increasing rather than reducing the involvement and participation of the people in government. And they fully understand the fundamental importance of checks and balances on power. In fact there is not much that divides real republicans and many constitutional monarchists. Constitutional monarchies are often among the most democratic states in the world.

Unlike the ARM, real republicans are not fixated on the crown. For example, Ted Mack, a leading new South Wales real republican has other concerns. While Mayor of North Sydney he successfully introduced Citizen Initiated Referenda. Opposed to the generous superannuation funds for MPs, he resigned from parliament, on two occasions, just before he would have become eligible for a pension. His real republicanism has a wider agenda of popular involvement in government but including direct election.

When the ARM indicated in the elections for the Constitutional Convention in 1998 that the direct election of the president by the people was a possibility, not only did they increase their vote, but they suggested that republican groups could achieve some consensus at the convention. That was not to be.

What were the origins of the convention? After Paul Keating had considered the 1993 report of the Republic Advisory Committee chaired by Malcolm Turnbull, he announced on 7 June 1995 his government's policy that Australia should become a republic by 2001. On the following day, the then leader of the opposition, John Howard, proposed a People's Convention. This had also been suggested by his predecessor Alexander Downer.

Although constitutional conventions had been crucial in the achievement of federation of Australia, none had been held in the twentieth century.

Until 1998 proposals for constitutional change came from governments, sometimes advised by specialist bodies. The Republic Advisory Committee, consisting only of republicans, and bound by its terms of reference to come up with a republican model, was the most partisan of these. Although often criticised for "manipulating" the process, the revival of the convention as an instrument for constitutional review was a democratic approach. And it was much more generous and fair to republicans than the former prime minister had been to monarchists and other constitutionalists.

The convention was made up equally of elected and nominated delegates. Some commentators suggested that because of the nominated delegates, the convention was stacked by the Howard government. This is untrue. A substantial number of places were reserved for nominees of the state and federal parliaments, which ensured a wide range of representation and of views. Many, if not the majority, turned out to be republicans.

It was made clear that if a republican model were adopted by the convention, it would be put to the people. Alternatively, there would be an indicative plebiscite offering choices.

The campaign that preceded the election of delegates demonstrated that there is no level playing field between the principal groups, the ARM and the ACM. The ACM estimates that the ARM outspent it in advertising by a factor of ten – about $5 or $6 million against $500,000.

The ARM was able to broadcast a large number of television advertisements. The ACM had none. In the voluntary postal ballot the ARM had the resources and the manpower of the ALP and ACTU behind it, evidenced by the high voting returns in safe Labor electorates. Many ALP MPs used their offices to mail out encouragement to voters. This was replicated by a few coalition MPs in favour of the ACM, but only in South Australia. And even then, the coalition MPs were divided, only some supporting the ACM. But the ACM led the vote in South Australia!

Apart from some small newspaper advertising, the ACM advertised on radio. Its campaign material was circulated by its own supporters – not by a compliant political party. Of the other groups, only Clem Jones' Queensland Republic Team advertised extensively.

ACM was warned that it could lag up to 20 per cent behind the ARM, such would be the effect of the ARM's advertising, the support it had enjoyed over the years of the Keating government, and its strong media backing.

In fact the ACM and its allies gained 30.67 per cent of the vote. The ARM obtained 30.34 per cent. Many of those who voted for ARM must have done so believing its claims that it would seriously countenance direct election. But soon after the convention opened, the ARM moved to close off any further discussion of direct election. This was too much for the independent republicans, who threatened a walk out. The ARM had to retreat and allow further discussion.

WHAT DID THE CONVENTION ACHIEVE?

This was the subject of a law forum, in the 1998 issue of the *University of New South Wales Law Journal*, Vol 4, No. 2 (UNSW). All of the following comments come from that journal, unless otherwise indicated.

Cheryl Saunders, a prominent academic lawyer said: "While some elected delegates had formerly been politicians, the convention generally broadened the range of people normally involved in the development of proposals for constitutional change."

Moira Rayner, a republican delegate, said: "It ran efficiently. It did not collapse, as it could have, on the second day. It got a result." Her final conclusion was, "We missed a chance in February."

Sir Harry Gibbs disagreed: "No doubt a constitutional convention should include representatives of all schools of political and constitutional thought, but the representation of sectional interests is more likely to divert attention from the constitutional issues than to assist in resolving them."

John Uhr, Director of Public Policy at Australian National

University, maintained that process was good even if the outcome wasn't:

The Convention was an important illustration of Australian democracy at work. An assessment of the worth of how the Convention went about its work can tell us much about the strengths and weaknesses of democracy in Australia ... As a process, the Convention proved valuable as an example of what can be achieved through wider community consultation over the agenda of government and closer public participation in government decision making. I remain sceptical about the enduring qualities of the final recommendation.

Yet Attorney-General Darryl Williams took a quite different view, which George Winterton explained is justifiable in terms of the government's purpose: "[Williams] recently declared the February 1998 Constitutional Convention 'an outstanding success'. This is a fair assessment if the convention is judged against its designated purpose – to decide whether Australia should become a republic, when this should occur, and which republican model would be put to referendum. However, at least for republicans, the convention will ultimately have failed unless a satisfactory model of republican government is approved at the referendum."

The convention soon demonstrated the vacuity of the terms republic and republicanism, at least as they are being used now in Australia.

Professor Greg Craven writes that whereas previously antipodean republicanism had tended to be perceived as a single, more-or-less uniform entity: "Now, however, we realise that there are at least three orders of republicanism."

Craven divides most of the republican delegates into one of three categories: "democratic republicans" or as he prefers to call them, "radical republicans"; "conservative republicans"; and "symbolic republicans", described by Craven as "mainstream republicans", and whom I have sometimes chosen to call "official republicans". Each group had its own claim to a kind of republicanism but some felt inclined to argue that theirs was the only legitimate expression of republicanism. As Moira Rayner explained: "The republican cause is a broad church. True believers may, and we did, legitimately differ, yet the Australian Republican Movement ... claimed orthodoxy and that other views were heretical."

Democratic Or Real Republicans

The democratic or real republicans were those delegates at the convention who embraced constitutional reform but saw it as not merely symbolic in nature. Rather, the symbol of a new political order was to gain its significance from the other substantive reforms that it heralded for the people. Many of these delegates combined to form a loose coalition, the "Direct Election of the President Group". But for many, a directly elected president transplanted into a Westminster system was not really enough. Often the aim was an executive presidency. These people were attempting to reform the system rather than merely redecorate it. They have united under the name "Real Republicans" to fight for a No vote in the 1999 referendum. They, even more than constitutional monarchists, attracted the ire of the official republicans. For example, the former Prime Minister Gough Whitlam called them "irresponsible and ignorant". (*Australian Financial Review*, 26 May 1999)

The democratic republicans were quickly robbed of any real opportunity to discuss their concerns. As John Uhr explains their predicament:

John Howard justified his Convention as a way of broadening the agenda of constitutional change from the head of state to other issues of great constitutional significance such as parliamentary terms, Commonwealth–State relations and the allocation of legislative and executive powers. Sadly, the Convention was given a much narrower brief, which pushed to the sides any constructive deliberation on related issues of democratisation and constitutional modernisation.

This was a great problem for those who, unlike the official republicans, were not interested merely in symbols. These included Moira Rayner and the Reverend Tim Costello. Rayner says: "We ... argued that the head of state was an unimportant symbol ... We had always said that the head of state issue was less important than our democratic and constitutional problems."

They were joined by a vocal minority, including Sydney Magistrate Pat O'Shane (who wanted not "just a republic" but "a just republic"), Western Australian Professor Patrick O'Brien and the teams mounted by former Brisbane Labor Lord Mayor Clem Jones in Queensland and former independent MP Ted Mack in New South Wales, to lobby for a directly elected president.

Discussion was not completely limited to minimalist change. John Uhr notes that much of the debate, and indeed the final communiqué, "strayed beyond these narrow confines" almost as a kind of proof that the popularly elected delegates would not be prevented from raising a wider range of issues for constitutional change.

Those hoping for reform, like Uhr, must remain profoundly disappointed with the convention's outcome. For this he blames a "sceptical" prime minister who had won a victory that promised to make an Australian republic safe for the prevailing interests who dominate Australian parliamentary government. "The preferred option leaves most of the crucial decisions in the hands of the ruling prime minister. Thus a conservative prime minister has the prospect of bringing home Labor's minimalist bacon." He seems to have forgotten John Howard is opposed to the model.

Richard McGarvie and the Conservative Republicans

The conservative republicans (perhaps we should call them "neo-monarchists") remained a force after the democratic republicans had been vanquished. This group comprised the delegates attracted to the model proposed by a former Victorian judge, then Governor Richard McGarvie. McGarvie acknowledged that the queen plays a real role in the constitution, one that a genuinely minimalist republican must seek to replace by a new institution.

They proposed to establish a council of retired statesmen and jurors, to appoint the president on the prime minister's advice.

Craven says that the conservative republicans have more or less "reluctantly" embraced the Australian republic as inevitable, but are vitally concerned to ensure that the new republic clings as closely as possible to the underpinnings of its monarchical ancestor. (Yet early in the referendum campaign Craven moved to support the so-called bi-partisan model that is the subject of the referendum – the second Keating–Turnbull republic.)

These are Australians who are willing to contemplate an Australian republic so long as it represents merely "an indigenous adoption" of Australia's highly successful system of constitutional monarchy.

Professor Winterton says that McGarvie is misguided in thinking that his constitutional council is any real substitute for the crown. He overlooks the important consideration that a head of state must enjoy "some legitimacy" for the effective performance of the functions of the offices, including both the symbolic role of national figurehead and focus for national unity and the exercise of reserve powers to protect the constitution if necessary. The governor-general's legitimacy derives from representation of the crown, which enjoys a legitimacy derived from history, tradition and sentiment and, for some, religion.

But, Winterton asks, what reserve of popular authority could a republican head of state chosen by a prime minister and appointed by a constitutional council draw upon when necessary to dismiss a prime minister or premier commanding the solid support of the lower house of parliament? Australia's political culture is, he says, "too egalitarian" to place much credence in a constitutional council of retired judges or retired heads of state. Moreover, while the "majesty and respect" enjoyed by the monarch may constrain an Australian prime minister in nominating a candidate for governor-general, it is difficult to envisage the proposed constitutional council fulfilling a similar function, so that the council's alleged equivalent with the monarch is "unsustainable". (*Adelaide Review*, August 1997)

Unlike the symbolic republicans, the conservative republicans are concerned about retaining the monarchical skeleton even if it is encased in a republican shell.

Professor Craven says that the existing system is not, as is sometimes supposed, unadulterated in character. Our democracy is fundamentally qualified. It is both "representative" and "parliamentary" in nature, so that the will of the people cannot legitimately be expressed directly and immediately, but only through the prism of their constitutionally elected representatives. This essentially conservative, British version of democracy was, he says, directly confronted at the convention by the "spectre of a popularly elected president" wielding popular power in defence of the electorate against its parliamentary representatives. So, he says, the real republicans were at odds with everyone who stood by a more traditional concept of Anglo-Australian constitutional theory. Craven suggests that the real dilemma for conservatives is one about how best to preserve the democracy they presently enjoy, rather than one about republicanism versus monarchy.

The conservative republicans exerted a greater influence over the official ARM republicans than the democratic republicans were able to do. This was principally because of a media campaign to tempt the ACM and its allies to vote "strategically". This strategy was to support the McGarvie model as the "least worst" republic, so it would emerge as the preferred model at the convention. The strategy then would be to campaign against the model at the referendum as the easiest one to defeat. The ARM would not believe ACM protestations that they were determined to resist this temptation. So they saw the need to win over at least some democrat republicans and conservative republicans by changing their model.

Official Republicans – the ARM

This group of republicans included the dominant voice at the convention, the Australian Republican Movement. The group differs from the conservative republicans (and to some extent the democratic or real republicans, too) by "ardently desir[ing] dramatic change in Australia's symbols". They differ also from the democratic republicans (and to some extent find common ground with the conservatives) by claiming not to seek to change the "substantive systems of government". The difficulty is that they either do not know what they are doing, or they are not letting on that they want to make significant changes to the constitution. For both of their models are substantially different from the present constitution.

Yet this is the school of the so-called "minimalists", the heirs to the Keating legacy. It had the numbers to largely control the republican vote at the convention provided the monarchists did not vote "strategically". The model endorsed by this group was the one that popped up in the last days with a nomination procedure tacked on as an apparent peace-offering for the democratic republicans, and an amended dismissal procedure to attract the conservative republicans and the Labor Party. In other words just another deal behind the scenes to get the maximum vote.

There are many critics of this group's final model. Professor Winterton, himself a delegate of the symbolic republic persuasion, explains that the convention's failings are largely attributable to two factors: insufficient attention was devoted to the details of the republican model, and the ARM conceded too much to the prime minister and to supporters of the McGarvie model in "a futile attempt" to secure their support.

Besides criticisms of their tactics, some highly informed commentators began to question the fundamental tenets of the minimalists' approach at the convention. Professor Cheryl Saunders has said that, in hindsight, minimalism was a mistake. It has encouraged Australians to think in terms of retaining unnecessary monarchical forms, while replacing the monarch.

This approach had resulted in a first model where the substance is monarchical and the symbolism republican. This is as intolerable to those who want substantial reform as it is to those who believe the existing machinery works well and should not be jeopardised. Moira Rayner writes that if the referendum succeeds we will enter the twenty-first century with "twentieth century amendments cobbled onto a nineteenth century constitution which is dressed up with a poetic, meaningless, preamble". She describes this as "the sweet smell of democratic decay masked with the synthetic scent of eucalyptus".

The official ARM republicans, despite their numbers, influenced few others. Their so-called symbolic changes were anything but that. They would work to the detriment of the existing system of checks and balances, which is so important to all other delegates! Furthermore they were unable to provide the kinds of reform desired by the democratic republicans. Their program did have initial appeal, however, for those people in society who sense the desirability of change, but have not yet considered the details or implications.

THE COMMUNIQUÉ

The convention's final resolutions were compiled into a communiqué given under the hand of the Chairman, Ian Sinclair, and the Deputy Chairman, Barry Jones, to the prime minister pending the compilation and tabling in parliament of a report of the convention.

In Principle Support for a Republic

The convention resolved that it supported "in principle, Australia being a republic".

This was hailed by republicans as a decisive victory. But as Sir Harry Gibbs points out, since there are many republican models, some of which may be attractive but others which would be regarded by Australians as entirely unacceptable, it is "futile to say that Australia should become a republic" unless an acceptable model for a republican constitution is at the same time suggested. A resolution drafted in the way this one was reflects sentimental preferences but covers up divisions. It was so lacking in meaning that every delegate could have, in good conscience, supported it.

The convention then resolved that the "Bipartisan Appointment of the President Model" be adopted "in preference to there being no change to the constitution" and, that the required changes "be put to the people in a constitutional referendum".

It was resolved that this referendum should be held in 1999, and if carried, the new republic should be instituted by 1 January 2001.

The States

The communique adopts a view never before advanced, that the crown is really seven crowns and that each can then be dismantled piece by piece. So the convention resolved that the commonwealth parliament and executive should consult their state counterparts to determine whether the adoption of a republican system by the central government would have any implications on the states' constitutional arrangements. It was also resolved that change at the commonwealth level should not pressure the states to make any involuntary changes and provision should be made to allow for any state that wished to retain their monarchical arrangements for the time being. All the states will not be required to change at the same time as the commonwealth.

As Sir Harry Gibbs explains, problems may arise from the convention's treatment of the states:

It would be absurd, and destructive of the symbolic significance which republicans attach to the change, if some states remained monarchies when the Commonwealth became a republic. Further, such a situation would give rise to constitutional questions as yet unresolved, including the question whether the change could be made without the assent of all states. It is a matter of controversy whether a referendum carried only in a majority of states would suffice for this purpose. On any view the *Commonwealth of Australia Constitution Act* (1900) would require amendment, and one view is that this could not be done by way of s128 of the Constitution. From every point of view, if Australia is to become a republic, the Commonwealth and the states should change together.

Julian Leser, the youngest convention delegate, warned that in a situation where a majority of votes is achieved overall and in the requisite four, but not all six, states, the high court may be required by the other two states to adjudicate on the constitutionality of the act. He says that the high court could be placed in "an invidious position". If it decided to make those declarations it would be forced to ignore the will of the majority of people, and the majority of people in four states. Conversely if it did not make those declarations it would force the two remaining states into a federal republic that they did not want – it would be ignoring the sovereignty of the people of those states. "The worst scenario for republicans who argue that a republic will bring Australians together is a high court challenge that will tear Australia apart." It should be noted that the high court cannot give an opinion on the constitutionality of proposed legislation in advance. (*In re Judiciary and Navigation Acts*, 1921, 29, CLR, 257)

The Bipartisan Model

This was the model that prevailed over the others, such as direct election or appointment by constitutional council on the prime minister's advice. It only had the support of 73 of the 152 delegates. It consists of four components: a nomination process; appointment by joint sitting of parliament; dismissal by the prime minister and; that the president's powers be those of the governor-general.

The Preamble

Going beyond its terms of reference, the convention resolved that a new preamble should be inserted in the constitution. The preamble to the Imperial Act is to remain, but any spent covering clauses are to be removed while any remaining operative will be moved into the constitution itself. This will presumably have the effect of limiting the content of the Imperial Act to the preamble, followed by the constitution, which will commence with a second preamble.

Eleven elements are stipulated for inclusion in the new preamble, ranging from a reference to "Almighty God" to an "affirmation of respect for our unique land and its environment". Three other matters are listed for possible inclusion. The most curious element is that the preamble is to be drafted "in such a way that it does not have implications for the interpretation of the constitution". As if that were not enough, Chapter II of the constitution (dealing with the Judicature) is to contain a new provision: "That the preamble not be used to interpret the other provisions of the constitution." It is not clear that this would be effective, especially in international forums.

On this Alex Reilly argues that it is illogical to support the expression of core values in a preamble, and then to ensure that they are not constitutionally enforceable: "In one breath the preamble pronounces values to aspire to, and in the next it ensures that those values are unenforceable in the interpretation of the constitution."

What was the intention? Mary Delahunty, an ARM delegate, described the preamble just as a "welcoming mat" for the constitution.

Craven suggests that some delegates had a more sinister intention. He says that the "constitutionally literate" among the radical republicans had no illusions about the process in which they were engaged. They hoped that the inclusion of rights and values in the preamble might provide "a right-minded high court" with a base from which to interpolate those concepts into the body of the constitution.

Sir Harry Gibbs is critical of the whole project, explaining that a constitution should prescribe the method of government, and an expression of social values is out of place in such an instrument.

It is particularly unwise to attempt to give constitutional recognition to contemporary values, since the most elementary knowledge of history should show how dramatically values can change in a comparatively short time ... It cannot be predicted with certainty whether those provisions would be used, with unpredictable results, in international tribunals as an indication of the principles which Australia, having recognised, should apply in practice.

Despite this, Winterton maintains that: "The convention's resolution on the preamble is one of its most significant, and least timid, accomplishments."

Even if not for Winterton's reasons, the preamble resolution is highly significant. It exhibits a desire to make sweeping gestures that have no substantive effect. But there was urgency and due attention was not paid to the detail – wherein the devil lies. In these senses, it seems to exhibit more transparently the symptoms present in the resolutions regarding the bipartisan model.

In any event, the convention's proposals were not accepted by the prime minister, who established a separate process, which will be the subject of a separate referendum.

Consequential Changes

The convention also passed resolutions on a number of consequential issues: the name "Commonwealth of Australia" be retained; the use of the title president; new oaths; commencement date of new provisions; various provisions regarding the presidency; provisions regarding monarchical symbols; and eligibility for the presidency.

It says that Australia will remain a member of the Commonwealth of Nations in accordance with the rules of the Commonwealth.

Ongoing Constitutional Review Process

The convention resolved that a provision be made for a mandatory convention to be held three to five years after the referendum is carried, with the purpose of reviewing "the operation and effectiveness of any republican system of government introduced by a constitutional referendum" and to address a broad range of issues. Irrespective of the desirability of another convention (there were many issues that could not be discussed at this one), making provision for reviewing the system is no compensation for getting it right the first time. If the 1999 referendum is carried, there is no reason to assume a subsequent referendum to correct the mistakes in the first one, would be carried. It will be hard enough to get one referendum through, let alone two.

National Symbols

Attention was drawn to the fact that although consideration of the Australian National Flag and Coat of Arms fell beyond the convention's terms of reference, some delegates raised the possibility of enshrining both in the constitution.

Definition of Presidential Powers

The convention effectively avoided this issue by resolving that the powers of the new head of state should be the same as those of the governor-general. To this end the constitution would spell out the non-reserve powers as far as practicable, and a new provision would be inserted stipulating that "the reserve powers and the conventions relating to their exercise continue to exist". This provides two problems, as we have seen. Firstly, the conventions of the crown could be less effective or disappear. Secondly, the new clause saving the conventions would effectively make them "justiciable" (ie reviewable by the court). As Sir Harry Gibbs observes:

If a provision to this effect is written into the Constitution, without qualifications, it will fall to the courts to decide what the constitutional conventions require. This would render an exercise of the reserve powers open to legal challenge, whereas at present those conventions are not open to judicial review.

So a constitutional crisis could drag on for months.

THE PROCESS AFTER THE CONVENTION

The Bipartisan Model was the result of the ARM trying to wrestle with great questions of constitutional law and political theory. It took no more than four days of discussion and negotiation, supported by many millions of dollars of taxpayers' funds. But it actually failed on the floor of the convention. Nevertheless, it was the preferred model of the republican delegates. Accordingly the prime minister decided that it should be put to the people in a referendum, a view supported by a majority of delegates and by all of the major political parties.

But in what form? Professor Winterton suggested that the "Parliament should *generally* honour the convention's resolutions". This is surely not good enough.

In a speech given on 27 March 1998, Sir David Smith warned against federal ministers changing the convention model in the parliament. The people should be allowed to vote on the republicans' preferred model:

(A)fter describing the final republican model as "a hybrid on a hybrid on a compromise" and after referring to elements of it which he believes are unworkable, Peter Costello was reported as vowing he will urge the Federal Parliament to amend the model produced by the Convention. Other reports spoke of Daryl Williams tinkering with the model during his Department's drafting of the referendum Bill. For the Government to allow the Treasurer and the Attorney to produce their own version of what they think the Constitutional Convention should have come up with, or for Parliament to tolerate such action, would be a betrayal of the Convention and a repudiation of the Prime Minister's undertaking. I hope that the community debate that lies ahead of us will be aimed at keeping the bastards honest.

8

THE SECOND
KEATING–TURNBULL REPUBLIC

We come now to the so-called "bipartisan model" for a republic that emerged from the Constitutional Convention.

It is essentially owned by the ARM, which had for years espoused the first version of the Keating–Turnbull republic. That is why it is best described as the second version of the Keating–Turnbull republic.

The fundamental question for Australians in the coming referendum is whether this model is better than, or at least as good as, the present constitution. The ARM argues that it is as good, and that the change is only symbolic. But if the ARM is questioned about the details of their model, the response usually is that opponents are engaged in the "*mother of all scare campaigns*". This will be a term used over and over during the campaign.

It is clear the last thing the ARM wants is a debate on the detail of the model. Kim Beazley says he would become "terribly depressed" if this debate were to be about the "minutiae" of the election of the president and the president's power. (*Australian*, 26 November 1998) The principal issue, he says, is about having an Australian head of state and a republic. Whether or not we like the process that emerges, he argues we can deal with any problems down the road. (*SBS* News, 27 January 1999) These could be fixed up at future referenda! These details should not cloud the move to a more "mature" political system. (*Australian*, 26 November 1998)

An unbiased observer could not fail to come to the conclusion that this is an admission the Keating–Turnbull republic is inferior to the present system. Kim Beazley's suggestion of further referenda confirms this.

But, surely, if a change of this nature is proposed – as Thomas Keneally says, the biggest structural change since Federation – we ought to end up with a constitution at least as good as we have. It is not as if there has not been enough time, or enough money spent. The taxpayers' money, not the ARM's.

In fact the ARM has had the best part of a decade, and by the referendum, about $120 million of the taxpayers' funds to produce their model and have it put to the people.

The first Keating–Turnbull republic was also a failure. It did not make the president a mirror image of the governor-general. It would have instead imported into Australia the essence of the 1958 French Fifth Republic, which allows the "cohabitation" between two powerful competing politicians, a president and a prime minister. The only reason France tolerates the inevitable tension between these two is that the dozen or so previous constitutions since 1789 were all failures too.

Displaying, as Sir Harry Gibbs says, a "remarkable pliability", the second Keating–Turnbull republic goes to the other extreme. It turns the president chosen by the politicians into the prime minister's poodle. And no explanation for this drastic change has ever been forthcoming. It bears all the marks of the frantic manoeuvring, wheeling and dealing, trade-offs and "back-of-the-envelope" drafting in the last days of the 1998 Constitutional Convention. All done just to achieve a majority of votes, which still eluded the ARM. The model puts the president at the absolute mercy of the prime minister. Unlike the constitution of any other democratic republic, the prime minister will be able to sack the president. At any time. For any reason. Or no reason. Without any notice or right of appeal. This is power that the prime minister certainly does not have now! To the question of why no other republic has such an arrangement, Clerk of the Senate Harry Evans gives the awesome answer. No other country has ever been so misguided as to accept such an obviously unbalanced arrangement. Leading experts on the constitution, most of them republican – have identified a multitude of serious flaws in this model.

The Australian public is passionate about fair play. A rule change which allows one of the captains to send off the referee will be recognised as the rort it so clearly is. This republican model is not only another embarrassing failure – it is dangerous.

To give effect to the model, two bills have been passed by both houses of parliament. They will not be submitted to the governor-general for the royal assent unless the principal bill, the *Constitutional Alteration (Establishment of Republic)* 1999, is approved in the referendum on 6 November 1999. The other bill is the *Presidential Nominations Committee Bill* 1999 *(Nominations Bill)*. The people can see this but not vote on it. Other significant areas of detail are also left to the politicians to develop and change.

The Referendum Question

The manner in which a referendum question is put to the people is governed by the *Referendum (Machinery Provisions) Act* 1984. A referendum question must set out the title of the proposed law to amend the constitution and then ask whether the voter approves.

The original title of the *Referendum Bill*, as introduced into parliament, read: "A Bill for an Act to alter the Constitution of Australia as a republic with a president chosen by a two-thirds majority of the members of the commonwealth parliament."

In its submission, ACM pointed out the long title does not refer to the unique and extraordinary aspect of the model. Unlike any other known republic, the prime minister can summarily dismiss the president. ACM therefore submitted that the following words be added to the title: "appointed for a term of five years but removable by the prime minister at any time by a signed notice with immediate effect".

Clerk of the Senate Harry Evans and ARM patron Senator Andrew Murray made similar submissions.

A range of submissions on the title were received by the

Parliament's Joint Select Committee on the Republic Referendum. At a hearing in Sydney on 5 July 1999, ARM Chairman Malcolm Turnbull even argued for the deletion of the words "republic" and "president". The Committee, whose membership was strongly republican, finally recommended the title be: "A Bill for an Act to alter the constitution to establish the Commonwealth of Australia as a republic, with the queen and governor-general being replaced by an Australian president." This was no improvement. It obviously excluded any reference to the method of choosing or especially dismissing the president. And while the president will replace the governor-general, the queen's functions certainly do not go to the president. They go to the politicians, particularly the prime minister. And the Committee wanted to state clearly and simply the essential purpose and outcome of the bill as it claimed, why did it put "Australian" before "president"? Surely the detail of the model is part of the essential purpose and outcome of the bill.

In the meantime polling had indicated that there would be substantially different results depending on the question. But it was probably not explained to those polled that all of the questions were in fact about the same model!

In any event the government chose an amended title which eventually prevailed: "A Bill for an Act to alter the Constitution to establish the Commonwealth of Australia as a republic with the queen and governor-general being replaced by a president appointed by a two-thirds majority of members of the commonwealth parliament."

The senate then approved an amendment by the Australian Democrats changing the title to: "A Bill for an Act to alter the Constitution to establish the Commonwealth of Australia as a republic." A meaningless title which the government rejected before both houses finally approved the bill.

Nomination

Under the *Nominations Bill*, any Australian citizen may nominate just about any other citizen to be president. This procedure is quite pointless. Under the *Nomination Bill* the 32-person

Presidential Nominations Committee, with a majority directly nominated or aligned to the prime minister, must give a confidential written report on nominations received, to the prime minister. This must include a confidential shortlist of the most suitable candidates (clause 20). The prime minister is not, under section 60, to do any more than consider the report. He may nominate any Australian citizen to be chosen as president. So why have this process? Before the convention election the ARM indicated it had not closed its mind on the question of direct election of the president by the people. They knew of course that opinion polls constantly show that if Australia were to become a republic, an overwhelming majority insist that the people should elect the president. So to camouflage the fact that the second Keating–Turnbull republic will be a politician's republic, we have a cosmetic nomination process.

And it may well be worse than useless.

Remember that Bill Hayden had said that only the "stout hearted" would be able to endure that "personal inquisition" to which a nominee might be subjected by a joint sitting of parliament.

As Sir Harry Gibbs says, this is likely to deter at least some suitable persons from allowing their names to be considered. (UNSW, 1998, 16) Those of the calibre of, say, Roma Mitchell, Zelman Cowan, Richard McGarvie, or Peter Sinclair are unlikely candidates.

We can be sure that this process will come to resemble US senate nominations, which in recent years have involved witch-hunts against anyone who is perceived as having ideas unacceptable to members of the relevant committee. At the convention, Federal Treasurer Mr Peter Costello said that the nominations process would put people who are up for consideration in a very difficult position. But when he put this to Malcolm Turnbull, who had come "like Nicodemus, by night to try to steal my vote". Mr Turnbull replied, "Don't worry about any of that: the parliament can ignore it." ("Hansard", 1998, 975)

Republican academic Professor John Williams writes that the untested political assumption is that the Nomination Committee will quell the people's obvious electoral appetite for a say in the election of the president.

He concludes that it is a hollow attempt to appease electoral demands in states other than NSW and Victoria. In other words, it's a front. And a failed one at that. It certainly hasn't fooled the real republicans, Ted Mack, Clem Jones, Phil Cleary and Martyn Webb.

The "Election"

The next stage in the process is for the prime minister to make a single nomination to a joint sitting of the commonwealth parliament. Under a last minute amendment it is only at this point that politicians and members of political parties are excluded. In other words they can resign just before nomination. The nomination must be seconded by the leader of the opposition in the house of representatives. The joint sitting must then approve the nomination by a two-thirds majority. So this will normally require approval by the opposition.

Winterton warns that it could be difficult to identify the leader of the opposition constitutionally, as the non-government parties in the lower house may have equal numbers, or no members at all – as was the case in New Brunswick after the 1987 election when the government won all the seats. His solution is to give this responsibility to the speaker of the house. The speaker is the neutral presiding officer, the symbol and advocate of the house as a whole. As such, he or she could not be entrusted with a political discretion. The speaker could be given the role only if it was not political, merely ceremonial. But in this case, the seconder has no choice but to second the nomination, further strengthening the position of the prime minister.

There seems to be no obligation on a prime minister to make a nomination. This could suit a prime minister who wishes to keep the office vacant, and is happy with the president continuing in office under section 61 or with an acting president or deputy president. Neither the support of the leader of the opposition, or of a joint sitting would be necessary to support this strategy.

As to the need for a two-thirds majority, Sir Harry Gibbs doubts whether, in a time of crisis, the political unanimity required by this procedure would be evident. This could be so especially after a dismissal of a president. Slovakia went without a president for months in 1998 because the parliament could not agree on whom to elect. (*Age*, 29 July 1998)

Craven, too, is aware of the problems that may arise when such a majority is not forthcoming: "Why are we to assume that a joint sitting of the two houses of the commonwealth parliament will produce the two-thirds majority necessary to appoint a president? What will happen if this does not occur? How can we be sure that debate in the joint sitting will not be used to publicly traduce presidential candidates under parliamentary privilege?"

Yet the requirement of a two-thirds by majority is presented as superior to the present process. It is suggested that this consensus or near consensus is a good thing. Those with experience know that it will be anything but that.

Bernard Levin, a noted British columnist once warned that:

It is a truth not sufficiently appreciated that any proposal which commands itself to both front benches is at best useless and at worst against the public interest. One which appeals to both parties' back benches is likely to be a constitutional outrage and certain to be seriously damaging to the people's liberty, prosperity or both.

To believe that opposition approval will be based solely on the virtues of the candidate suggests a high degree of naivete. That is just not how the political world operates. Clerk to the Senate Harry Evans explains what in fact will happen:

The prime minister would have to put forward a nominee acceptable to the other major party, which implies that consultations would take place before the nomination is made. Consultations among politicians lead to deals. The deal may be for a candidate acceptable to both parties and not likely to offend any major strand of opinion in either party. A lowest-common-denominator effect could well set in. Recent appointees as governor-general might not have passed muster in such a party agreement. A political deal can also take the form of a trade-off. An opposition may well accept the government's nominee on the basis of some returned favour. The deal could be: We do not really like your presidential nominee, but we will support the nomination if you will do something in return for us.

Public negotiations also tend to leak. The way in which the presidential nominee has been selected would inevitably become known to the public. The deals would be explained in the press. The selection process would then be looked upon unfavourably by outsiders and demeaning to the candidate selected.

Of course, politicians are well accustomed to deals. Northern Territory Chief Minister Mr Shane Stone argued that even on the subject of the proposed law to suppress the Northern Territory euthanasia law, a conscience vote was impossible. "What you'll see is the linking up of groups in factions, deals will be done and there'll be trade-offs with people . . . in the senate in exchange for other bills. I know how it works, we're a soft target, we're an easy trade." (*Sydney Morning Herald*, 6 July 1996)

Perhaps one of the best known deals was the Kirribilli House Agreement made before the 1990 election.

Prime Minister Hawke agreed that after the election, and unbeknown to the electors, he would hand over the prime ministership to Paul Keating. Witnessed by TNT CEO Sir Peter Abeles and ACTU Secretary Bill Kelty, the agreement was kept secret. But when Mr Hawke changed his mind after the election and Mr Keating went to the backbench to campaign against him, the agreementfound its way to the press. (Hawke, 451–453)

The point was of course that the deal was of momentous public interest. The people thought they were electing a government to be led by Bob Hawke, not Paul Keating. It is of course either naive or deceptive to think that politicians will use the power to elect a president only for the purpose of choosing a president above politics. The two-thirds vote will ensure that they enter into a series of deals and trade-offs as the price for accepting the prime minister's nomination. The Americans understood this. So when they founded their republic, they wanted to ensure that the process of electing the president was not corrupted by deals and trade-offs. The politicians were totally excluded from the process, especially re-elections, to ensure, as founder Alexander Hamilton insisted, there was no "sinister bias". (Hamilton, 457)

But in Australia the political deals and trade-offs surrounding the election of the president will not only be possible, they will be entrenched.

The president will owe his office to politicians' deals. Worse, he is just as likely to be a party to the deals. Yet the ARM argues that popular election will inevitably produce a politician. Their president will not only be a politician, but one who emerges from shabby and secret political deals. As democratic republican Ted Mack says, "The president won't be one of us. He'll be one of them." This will no longer be a position beyond politics. The second Keating–Turnbull republic will most certainly be a politician's republic. And the president will most definitely be *the politicians' president.*

The President

A new section 59 of the constitution would provide that:

The executive power of the Commonwealth is vested in the president and extends to the execution and maintenance of this Constitution, and of the laws of the Commonwealth. The president shall be the head of state of the Commonwealth.

There shall be a Federal Executive Council to advise the president in the government of the Commonwealth, and the members of the Council shall be chosen and summoned by the president and sworn as Executive Councillors, and shall hold office during the pleasure of the president.

The president shall act on the advice of the Federal Executive Council, the prime minister or another minister of state; but the president may exercise a power that was a reserve power of the governor-general in accordance with the constitutional conventions that related to the exercise of that power by the governor-general.

It will be noted that for the very first time the term "head of state" is to appear in an Australian constitutional document. This is a diplomatic term which has been used, or more correctly misused, by the ARM to create a case for change. This totally superfluous provision can have been inserted only to give some substance to the deception that the governor-general is not already a head of state and that the term is of some constitutional significance, which it is clearly not.

The first and second paragraphs continue, in a republican form, sections 61 and 62 of the existing constitution. However, the third paragraph differs both from the present constitution, and also from the Communiqué of the Constitutional Convention in two ways.

First, the sources of advice to the president specified in the constitution are increased from the present one, the federal executive council. The sources of advice are now the federal executive council, the prime minister or another minister of state.

Although the addition of the prime minister and another minister of state to the federal executive council actually reflect current constitutional practice, their express inclusion creates a situation where the president may receive conflicting advice of apparently equal validity from different sources. This would not matter if such advice were not legally binding, which is the position at present.

The second difference is the more important. The president is now legally bound to act on advice. This appears to deny the president the traditional rights of the governor-general to be consulted, to advise, and to warn. That is, as a constitutional auditor.

Thus, if any minister of state insisted that he act immediately, the president would probably be precluded from doing what governors-general have normally done – asked questions, requesting the executive council to obtain formal advice from the attorney-general or solicitor-general, or delay acting on questionable advice until satisfied that it was constitutional or legal. The Constitutional Convention did not recommend that the president be placed under a binding legal obligation to act on advice. We have previously referred to the case in India, where Mrs Ghandi had insisted the president sign an unjustified Declaration of Emergency. Under this constitution, a president could not refuse.

It is difficult to exaggerate the enormity of the change. At one stroke it denies the president the day-to-day power and duty that governors-general have enjoyed as auditors of proper process since federation.

But that is not all. The reference to the reserve powers appears to make their exercise *justiciable* – that is, reviewable in the high court, a matter ACM raised soon after the *Exposure Draft* was released in April 1999.

The reserve powers are those where the governor-general may act on his own discretion as the constitutional umpire.

Under the third paragraph of the new section 59 we have a tension. There is now a mandatory obligation on the president to act in accordance with the advice of the executive council and others. But there is an exception relating to the exercise of the reserve powers in accordance with the constitutional conventions governing their exercise by the governor-general. As the first part of this paragraph imposes a legal duty on the president, ACM and others argued it would be "justiciable" and thus enforceable in the high court. (See for example the high court decision in *The Queen vs Toohey, ex parte Northern Land Council*, 1981, 151, CLR 170) So the exercise of a reserve power must also be "justiciable". The traditional view is that the exercise of the reserve powers under the present Australian constitutions cannot be examined or reviewed by the courts. For example, Sir John Kerr's decision to dismiss Mr Whitlam and dissolve parliament could not have been reviewed by the high court.

Some Australian jurists say the law has developed so that now the exercise of the reserve powers is justiciable.

On this view, Sir John Kerr's decision to dismiss Gough Whitlam in 1975 could have been reviewed by the high court. That could have extended the constitutional crisis for many weeks or even months. This was the Pakistan experience when the exercise of the president's powers were found to be justiciable.

In the absence of a clear provision in the constitution, only the high court can give us the answer. And then only when someone with standing seeks a review.

More recently the former solicitor-general and attorney-general, republican Bob Ellicott QC, dropped a bombshell. He argued that it was likely that the high court would find that under the Keating–Turnbull republic the president had actually lost the power to dismiss the prime minister. This flowed from the proposed new section 59, which provides that the president may exercise a power that was a reserve power of the governor-general "in accordance with the constitutional conventions" relating to the exercise of that power.

But the attorney-general says in the Republic Bill Explanatory Memorandum, referring to 1975, that there is no generally agreed convention relating to the exercise of the reserve powers. New section 59 only allows the president to exercise a reserve power in accordance with convention.

Ellicott concludes that if a president dismissed a prime minister under this republic the high court could review the president's decision, but guided by the Explanatory Memorandum, it could then find the power to dismiss no longer existed.

Just before the Republic Bill was to be passed in August 1999, the attorney-general introduced an amendment. Under clause 8 of schedule 3, the bill will not make justiciable the exercise of a reserve power if the exercise is not justiciable now. But as we have seen the law is now unclear on this point. And because of the "who shoots first scenario" which we are yet to discuss, high court involvement may be unavoidable. It would have been far better to have closed off the potential for a high court review of the president's exercise of a reserve power. After all, the exercise of the prime minister's power to dismiss the president is not reviewable. Why should the president's? This is yet another example of the failure of the Keating–Turnbull process to involve the people at all stages, and to ensure proper public discussion. It once again demonstrates that this model has been scrambled together without the careful consideration which was a feature of the federation process.

DISMISSAL

All democratic republics give the president a degree of tenure during his or her term. Where he or she presides over a Westminster system the president will ideally operate as a check and balance on the politicians. If she or he does not, then you have a system that leaves the same politicians in control of both the legislature and the government – an excessive and dangerous concentration of power.

Historical evidence demonstrates that in the Westminster system the crown, rather than a president, provides the better check and balance as an umpire and auditor against this concentration of power. (Obviously there are others, the courts, a free press etc.)

A Westminster president needs to have a clearly defined role. His powers must be codified – which, as we have seen, can bring in the problem of justiciability. How do we know the precise boundaries of his powers without a court ruling on them? And above all the president needs security of tenure, but obviously he or she should be removable for proven and serious breaches of the law or of her duties.

This is normally done through a three-stage process of impeachment. First there is a formal charge or impeachment on specified facts falling within grounds for dismissal set out in the constitution. So that this is not frivolously made, this usually has to satisfy, say, a house of parliament, as in the United States, or a specified majority of members of parliament. Then there is a fair trial. For example, before the senate as in the US, or before a tribunal of five judges presided over by the chief justice, as in Singapore.

Finally, there is usually a parliamentary vote with a special majority (two-thirds in the US, three-quarters in Israel and Singapore).

Without an impeachment process you cannot have a democratic republic.

The eerie words of the proposed new section 62 of the constitution demonstrate that this is not a democratic republic: "The prime minister may, by instrument signed by the prime minister, remove the president with effect immediately."

These are words which have no precedent in any constitution of any republic.

The prime minister must seek approval from the house of representatives for this action within thirty days unless, (i) within the thirty days the house expires or is dissolved or, (ii) before the removal, the house has expired or dissolved, but a general election has not taken place. Note that the senate is not involved. Sir Anthony Mason thinks this goes too far in strengthening the house against the senate. The exclusion of the senate is especially significant in the light of the 1975 crisis. Had Sir John Kerr been a president under this republic, Gough Whitlam would have been able to instantly dismiss him without any reference to the senate.

But if the house of representatives does not ratify the prime minister's action, the president is not to be re-instated. According to the Explanatory Memorandum, this ensures an opportunity for parliamentary scrutiny of the prime minister's action. This is not so, it only allows for scrutiny by the house.

The Explanatory Memorandum recalls that the convention had said a failure by the house of representatives to ratify the prime minister's decision to dismiss the president would constitute a vote of no confidence in the prime minister. The Memorandum says it is highly unusual to have a vote of no confidence in a single minister, particularly the prime minister. One consequence of a vote of no confidence in the prime minister might be loss of government. However, the constitution is silent on the issue. So it leaves the question unresolved. It is to be left "for resolution in accordance with parliamentary processes, which must in turn develop within the broader constitutional framework". Whatever that may mean. Yet another example of how little proper care and scrutiny has been given to this model.

Sir Harry Gibbs believes that just the knowledge of his own insecurity would prevent a president from taking valuable but uncontroversial initiatives. He recalls the decision taken in Tasmania in 1989 by Governor Sir Phillip Bennett, who would not accede to the request of the premier that an election be held. The governor was satisfied that the opposition could form a government with the support of the Greens. The model, Sir Harry says, fails completely to strike a balance between the offices and greatly strengthens the position of the prime minister at the expense of the president.

A long list of criticisms is levelled against the procedure by Professor Winterton, some of which include: failure to stipulate grounds for removal; unnecessary exclusion of the senate from the dismissal procedure; the prime ministerial action may be thwarted by pre-emptive presidential action; failure to explain why a wrongly removed president should not be automatically re-instated; and presidential competency should not be linked to the house's confidence in the prime minister.

Gareth Evans, a minister in the Keating government and a prominent republican delegate at the Constitutional Convention, has been quoted as saying he could never live with having a president who could be dismissed by the prime minister at the stroke of a pen – that this would make our president the most miserable head of state in the world. (Frank Devine, *Australian*, 12 February 1999)

Both Keating–Turnbull republics suffer from the fundamental deficiency that while they would dismantle the crown piece by piece, first federally and then at the state level, they offer nothing in its place. It is difficult not to come to the conclusion that the ARM just does not understand the role and nature of the Australian crown. Not understanding, they wish to destroy that institution, without putting anything in its place – except the absolute executive authority of the prime minister.

The proposition that the neutered office of president could be an adequate substitute for the crown confirms an inability or unwillingness to accept the subtleties of the present constitutional arrangements. The second Keating–Turnbull republic ensures that the president must emerge from deals and trade-offs between the politicians under this system. He is already guaranteed to be the politician's president. But this politician's president will hold office at the whim of the prime minister.

Anglo-American political thought and practice is suspicious of the proposition that an ideal political arrangement can be devised, and that the government established should be endowed with vast powers. Rather, our tradition is to be suspicious of potential abuses of power. This is reflected in the advice of Paul Keating's own Republic Advisory Committee, chaired by Malcolm Turnbull. They reported they had encountered an almost universal view that, regardless of the integrity of any prime minister, the head of state should not hold office at the prime minister's whim, and must be safe from instant removal to ensure appropriate impartiality. The need to protect the head of state from arbitrary removal has particular force, they said, where the head of state has discretionary powers that can be exercised adversely to the interests of the prime minister or the government. (RAC, Vol 1, 77)

The traditional view is most famously enunciated in Lord Acton's dictum, "Power tends to corrupt, and absolute power corrupts absolutely." Thomas Jefferson once asked, "What has destroyed liberty and the rights of men in every government?" He answered: "The concentration of all powers into one body." And as we have noted, ARM patron Senator Andrew Murray warns that the second Keating–Turnbull republic gives the prime minister "absolute executive power".

When confronted with this the proponents of the Keating–Turnbull republic nowhere acknowledge their previous counsels against the president holding office at the whim of the prime minister. Their knee-jerk reaction is to talk of the "mother of all scare campaigns". But when pressed they answer the critique in three ways – and thereby accept that the fault exists. First, they say, no reasonable person would behave so unreasonably. Then they say that the prime minister will not be able to choose "the president's successor". Finally they claim that it merely replicates the current system.

No prime minister would dismiss unreasonably

But people in power do not always act "reasonably". Emeritus Professor Geoffrey Blainey, in a speech on 10 March 1998, reminded us that in the 1930s one of the world's most civilised countries, Germany, fell into dictatorship because at the very top the constitutional checks and balances of the Weimar Republic were found wanting. Of course he was not saying, as one newspaper suggested, that another Hitler is possible. What he was reminding us was to those who say that authoritarianism could never come, one of the principal purposes of a constitution should be to ensure that excessive concentrations of power are not possible.

During the convention debates of the nineteenth century, Sir Richard O'Connor actually warned of the dangers of a supply crisis particularly where a double dissolution was not available. But the founders preferred to rely on the good sense and moderation of politicians rather than a special provision to cover this. (Galligan, 85,86) In 1975, good sense and moderation seemed to have flown the coop. It was fortuitous that the "trigger" existed for a double dissolution. If it had not, the governor-general could still have acted, but only by having a dissolution of the house of representatives and an election for half the senate. The new Senators, with the exception of those from the territories, would not have taken office for many months.

What good would dismissal do the prime minister?

The ARM's second response is that in dismissing the president the prime minister will not necessarily get his man or woman as acting president. Won't he? The *Republic Bill* makes it clear that the prime minister can dismiss any or all acting presidents, and that the prime minister could already have such deputy presidents as he wishes, with such powers as he has specified. Proposed section 63 of the constitution assures this:

63 Acting President and deputies:

Until the Parliament otherwise provides, the longest-serving state governor available shall act as president if the office of president falls vacant.

A state governor is not available if the governor has been removed (as acting president) by the current prime minister under section 62.

Until the Parliament otherwise provides, the prime minister may appoint the longest-serving state governor available to act as president for any period, or part of a period, during which the president is incapacitated.

The provisions of the constitution relating to the president, other than sections 60 and 61, extend and apply to any person acting as president.

Until the parliament otherwise provides, the president may appoint any person, or any persons jointly or severally, to be the president's deputy or deputies, and in that capacity to exercise during the pleasure of the president (including while the president is absent from Australia) such powers and functions of the president as the president thinks fit to assign to such deputy or deputies; but the appointment of such deputy and deputies shall not affect the exercise by the president personally (including while the president is absent from Australia) of any powers or functions . . . (These powers are exercised on "advice": section 59)

We have thus the most extraordinary aggregation of power in the hands of the prime minister ever known in the history of our country, or indeed of any democracy. This results from the following:

- The prime minister's unprecedented power to dismiss the president.
- The extension of this power even further, in ways not envisaged in the convention model, by giving the prime minister a further unprecedented power to engage in the "serial dismissal" of those acting presidents he does not want.
- The fact that the constitutional provisions about acting presidents and deputy presidents may be changed without any reference to the people by an ordinary act of parliament. Again, none of this was provided for in the convention model.
- The prime minister is to be the sole judge of the president's *incapacity. He doesn't even need a medical certificate.*

- The president can be required by the prime minister to appoint any number of deputy presidents with such powers as the prime minister advises.
- The power of the prime minister to delay a new appointment indefinitely, thus keeping a crony president or acting president in office, or even having none.

The result is that the role of the president, as a check and balance on unconstitutional action by the prime minister, is weakened even further than in the 1998 convention communiqué. *The politician's president will be well and truly the prime minister's apathetic poodle.*

The prime minister can do it now

The ARM's final attempt to answer concerns about the prime minister's extraordinary concentration of power in this republic is to claim that he will have no more than the prime minister enjoys now. That this is untrue can be demonstrated by reference to the events of 1975.

Sir John Kerr says that on 11 November 1975 he asked Gough Whitlam if he intended to govern without supply. When Whitlam replied that he did, Sir John said he intended to withdraw Whitlam's commission. Whitlam jumped up, looked at the telephone and said: "I must get in touch with the palace." "It is too late," Sir John said. Whitlam asked "Why?" Sir John told him: "Because you are no longer prime minister; these documents tell you so, and why."

In a re-run of 1975, it would be possible under this republic for Gough Whitlam instead of saying: "I must get in touch with the palace," to have simply dismissed him.

He could have scribbled and signed a note saying: "You're dismissed." Under this republic he may well carry a prepared note. The point is there is nothing – nothing Gough Whitlam could have done to have secured Sir John Kerr's dismissal at their meeting on 11 November 1975.

It is completely untrue to say that the instant dismissal under the Keating–Turnbull republic replicates our current system. The procedure for the appointment and, by implication, the removal of governors-general was in fact settled at the Imperial Conference in 1930 where it was agreed that formal advice on an appointment (and thus removal) would come from the dominion ministers, usually the prime minister. But this would be after informal consultation. All of which takes time. It is true that the prime minister can *recommend* to the queen the removal of the governor-general. But that does not equate to the governor-general holding office at the whim of the prime minister.

In 1932 prime minister de Valera petitioned the king to dismiss the governor-general of the Irish Free State. The king did feel some doubt about whether he had to accept de Valera's advice. He declared that, while he was ready to act in accordance with constitutional practice respecting advice, in this case the advice was related to the position of the sovereign and to his personal prerogative and, therefore, the advice had a special character. So he asked for reasons to be given for de Valera's request. He also wanted Governor-General McNeill to be given an opportunity to resign and a longer period of notice. In this case, the King's decision had the effect of inducing a voluntary relinquishment of office and so obviated the need for the King to exercise his prerogative.

How might this compare with the situation that could have arisen in 1975 had Whitlam attempted to act as de Valera did? Whether or not one believes the queen would have been bound to act on such a request, it is clear that Sir John Kerr would not have been dismissed immediately on the basis of a midnight telephone call. Even if he had wanted to, which he denies, Gough Whitlam could not have had the governor-general dismissed in time to evade his own dismissal. In 1982 the queen's private secretary, Sir William Heseltine, confirmed this in a letter later cited at a session of the Advisory Committee of the Australian Constitutional Commission: "I can say that, while a telephone call from the prime minister might have frozen the situation, Her Majesty certainly could not have acted on the basis merely of a telephone conversation to dismiss her governor-general. Some formal instrument, whether transmitted by mail or cable, would most certainly have been required." And Sir David Smith points to the recent New Guinea example, where an original document, not a facsimile, was apparently thought necessary.

Professor George Winterton a professor of constitutional law, and a republican, accepts that the queen could take time to consider any advice of the prime minister and even endeavour to persuade the prime minister to withdraw his advice. He says the queen would ultimately "be obliged to accede to that advice unless she were willing to countenance a general election in which her conduct was an issue". He accepts that under the Keating–Turnbull republic the president will lack "this slender shield" and that the president's vulnerability will be "unprecedented among world republics". (*Weekend Australian*, 7–8 August 1999)

Fred Daly, who was the Leader of the House and Minister for Administrative Services at the time of the 1975 crisis, agrees and he ought to know. He confirms that the removal of a governor-general is not a speedy or simple process. (Daly, 237) Sir Anthony Mason believes that any assumption that the queen would act immediately on a prime minister's request is "quite incorrect". He believes that the queen would be entitled to consider the matter. She might well take the view that an Australian constitutional controversy should take its course according to the judgement of the governor-general "without intervention on her part until that controversy was resolved". (Mason, 1998)

Author Sarah Bradford writes that while there is nothing the queen can do if a prime minister submits a name for appointment she is not happy with, she is not powerless. She recounts a story about a Dean of St Paul's who had asked what the queen could do if she received advice to make an unsatisfactory ecclesiastic appointment. The queen replied, "I can always say I should like more information. This is an indication a prime minister will not miss." (Bradford, 498)

But the strongest argument against the proposition that the governor-general holds office at the prime minister's whim comes from Gough Whitlam himself. He suggests the proposition is "preposterous" and "ludicrous"! In *The Truth of the Matter* he ridicules Sir John Kerr's fears that he could have him removed by telephone. Whitlam referred to our recent experience in seeking the removal of Queensland Governor Sir Colin Hannah's "dormant" commission to act as administrator of the common-wealth. All state governors normally receive these. Sir Colin had publicly criticised the Whitlam government, that it engaged in political controversy – an act normally thought to be incompatible with viceregal status. An open and shut case for removal. It took ten days.

Whitlam says he merely asks: "Have you discussed this with the palace?" and that Kerr replied, "I don't have to and it's too late for you. I have terminated your commission."

At the very least then, even if she ultimately accepted her prime minister's advice, the queen would be entitled to the three rights recognised by the celebrated nineteenth-century constitu-tional authority Bagehot: to be consulted, to encourage, and to warn. That means time, precious time.

As we have seen some experts say the queen has a discretion to refuse unacceptable advice. Professor Tony Blackshield and Justice Kim Santow say it is generally accepted that if in 1975 there had been a race to the queen and Gough Whitlam had won, the queen would have exercised an independent discretion in deciding whether to remove the governor-general in what were already exceptional circumstances. (*Australian Financial Review*, 16 February 1998) However, those who have been closest to the question, Sir John Kerr and Sir David Smith, think that ultimately the queen must accept the prime minister's advice if he insists.

In any event, as former governor-general (and Labor Premier of New South Wales) Sir William McKell has pointed out, there is no guarantee as to when she will act. Sir William said that the queen is a very busy woman. She may be difficult to contact. She can always ask for more information. So by the time she acts the governor-general could have ensured an election takes place.

Indeed, the very idea that a prime minister could be automatically granted the removal of a governor virtually negates the reserve powers of the governor-general. Governors-general would be all but powerless if they could be removed any time they resisted the prime minister's will.

Who shoots first?

At this point we refer to a curious feature of this hurriedly put together constitution. Yet another example of the lack of care, and the need for public discussion in the drafting of such an important document. This is the practical difficulty of both the president being able to dismiss the prime minister and the prime minister being able to dismiss the president. This has just not been thought through. Who moves first will be absolutely crucial. Would a prudent president and prime minister carry signed notices of dismissal to future meetings, might either of them even backdate a notice of dismissal? There is not even the need for a witness on the prime minister's notice! If they met alone there could be different recollections of what had happened.

Hadn't the authors of this considered what had actually happened in 1975? Because in 1975 Gough Whitlam and Sir John Kerr had different recollections of the events in the study at Yarralumla.

Sir John's claim that Gough Whitlam rose, looked at the phones and said, "I must get in touch with the palace," Whitlam denies. He says:

This is a concoction and an absurd one. I had been in the governor-general's study at least half a dozen times when Lord Casey was governor-general and scores of times while Sir Paul Hasluck and Sir John Kerr had been governors-general. While Sir Paul and Sir John had made telephone calls and received them while I was there, I had no knowledge of the procedure for making calls. I did not know the number of the Palace. I had no staff with me. He had his aides, his secretaries, his telephonists, and his police. I was trapped in an ambush; my sole instinct was to escape, to depart at once from the place where the deed had been done and the presence of the man who had done the deed.

So Sir John Kerr says that Gough Whitlam was about to telephone the queen to have him dismissed, and Gough Whitlam denies this. At a meeting in a similar crisis and under this republic, establishing who moved first could be equally disputed.

The former Chief Justice Sir Anthony Mason worries about the ability of either to sack the other in a "who shoots first" scenario. Professor Cheryl Saunders writes that this ludicrous situation is, to say the least, undignified.

In the event of both claiming to have dismissed the other first, the president would appoint a new prime minister, and the old prime minister would have the acting president he wanted. In other words two claiming to be prime minister and two claiming to be president and, it should be stressed, two claiming to be commander-in-chief. That the phenomenon of two or more persons claiming to be president has happened in other countries is surely a good argument not to adopt a half-baked constitutional model that would allow this to be repeated here.

Republican critics

It is not surprising that this model has been criticised by constitutional experts, many of them republicans. The following come from the 1998 *University of New South Wales Law Journal Forum*:

The convention's model is flawed. Its presidential removal mechanism is both structurally unsound and entirely inappropriate. *Professor George Winterton*

I remain sceptical about the enduring qualities of the final recommendation for the so-called bipartisan appointment model. *Professor Cheryl Saunders*

It is a weak model, with a number of serious deficiencies. *Professor Greg Craven*

This model does not prevent a politically motivated dismissal of a president. *Professor Linda Kirk*

In summary, the conclusion must be that the extraordinary unprecedented power to remove the president is unknown in any democratic republic. And in no way does it replicate our existing system.

AND THE CONSEQUENCES?

The model, let us remember, is not based on carefully considered, dispassionate and extended discussion. It was scrambled together in the last few days to get the maximum support at the convention. It is full of holes. The most worrying aspect is the failure of its proponents to admit now that it is a model unworthy of our great democracy. Remember that the ARM refused to admit, for five years, that the first Keating–Turnbull republic was a recipe for instability. We have to assume that by now the proponents must be well aware of the fundamental and dangerous concentration of power, and the potential for instability that flows from this model.

Real republican former independent MP Ted Mack says many in the ARM, the media and academia are well aware of this. (*Sydney Morning Herald*, 24 December 1998)

And success in the referendum will result in pressure for other changes, apart from those changes that could occur because of a failure to prepare for them properly, such as on our membership of the Commonwealth of Nations.

Certainly the flag, the chief national symbol, is next on the agenda. As Bill Hayden has said, if the referendum is successful, "the same gang of activists will be on the campaign trail to change the flag".

The states too are on the agenda. A minister in the Keating government, Alan Griffiths, pointed this out at the beginning when he said: "The republican issue is a threshold thing, to get people's attention ... the real business was achieving competitiveness in government arrangements which might, in the long run, entail the abolition of the state. (*Australian Financial Review*, 5 April 1993)

But the worst consequences may be those which could flow from governmental instability that the model allows.

As we have seen, a president and a prime minister can sack each other. The president could say his dismissal was invalid or his was first and appoint the opposition leader as prime minister. An acting president could claim to be in office. There would be challenges in the high court that would inevitably become politicised. In the turmoil, with increasing civil disorder, both "presidents" (and perhaps both prime ministers) could call on the Army for support. Whom should the Army obey?

Eventually, supply would run out, with government services and payments curtailed. This scenario wasn't dreamt up as part of a "scare campaign". It comes from the experiences of other countries that have drafted or changed their constitutions without thinking carefully about the consequences. Pakistan has actually lived through similar events over the last years.

So it would obviously be more difficult under the Keating–Turnbull republic to resolve a 1975-style crisis. It would have far more serious consequences.

In 1975, the Australian economy was cordoned off from the world. Now all the regulatory barriers are down. As Paul Keating discovered a decade ago when in the course of warning about the state of the economy on talk-back radio, he uttered just two words, "banana republic". Foreign money was flushed out of Australia and international confidence collapsed. The dollar plunged.

Australia cannot afford the luxury of constitutional instability. The resulting international judgement would be harsh and immediate. As the dollar crashed, as Standard and Poor and Moody's reassessed their rankings most Australians would be the losers. The only people standing to gain would be speculators on our currency and those who buy up our property cheaply.

So the cost of this republic would not only be the $120 million to get to the referendum. It will not only be the hundreds of millions to change the currency, the uniforms, to upgrade everything; to pay for the president, deputy presidents, and the state presidents, who both in office and retirement with their new status will expect to be maintained in greater style than our retired governors and governors-general. It will be the cost to the nation of giving up its constitutional stability.

Australians are being engulfed with the argument that this change is only symbolic, only about an Australian head of state.

That is not what it is about. It is not only about getting rid of the queen at any price, it is about a major transfer of power in Australia.

9

REFERENDA, PLBISTES AND OPINION POLLS

One of the several remarkable features of the Australian constitution is that, unlike the Canadian, it was immediately repatriated to Australia. "Repatriation" is a term which Prime Minister Pierre Trudeau slipped into Canadian political debate, just as Paul Keating did with the term head of state in Australia. Canada had to wait many decades after Australia to enjoy repatriation. This only came in 1982. (Repatriation is the power to amend your own constitution.) The barrier to the Canadians enjoying this before 1982 was not British imperialism. It was the failure of the Canadians to agree on a formula for constitutional amendment. It was the bulldozing through of repatriation by an impatient Trudeau that ignited three decades of constitutional turmoil in Canada. A good lesson in not ramming through constitutional change.

Section 128 of our constitution allows Australians the power of amendment. But not only were Australians to be allowed to change their own constitution from 1901, any such change had to be approved by the people. Most other Constitutions until then set up special procedures for constitutional amendment. But this invariably only required approval by the politicians, by special majorities, or through elected conventions.

The Australian constitutional founders took the concept of the referendum from Switzerland. They surrounded the referendum procedure with quite tight restrictions. A proposed law to change the constitution had to be passed by an absolute majority in each house of parliament, and then put to the people. (Where the houses do not agree, it is still possible for the governor-general to submit the referendum to the people.)

Not only is a national majority of electors voting required for a referendum proposal to succeed, there must also be a majority of those voting in a majority of states. That is, four states out of the six. If so approved, the proposed bill is then presented to the governor-general for royal assent.

A majority of electors voting in a state is necessary to approve any alteration:

- diminishing the proportionate representation of that state in either house.
- diminishing the minimum number of representatives of that state in the house of representatives (the most relevant is the minimum for Tasmania of five).
- increasing, diminishing, or otherwise altering the limits of that state.
- in any manner affecting the provisions of the constitution in relation to that state.

Australia's referendum procedure and its record in approving constitutional change has been much criticised. But, as political scientist Professor Brian Galligan points out, comparisons with say, the Swiss record, fail to take into account the fact that referenda in Australia can *only* be initiated by the federal parliament. Hence they have been mainly concerned with giving the federal parliament more powers. Republicans outside of the ARM – "real republicans" – are typically concerned with making the Australian constitutional system more responsive to the popular will. Should the referendum in November 1999 fail, it is likely that the real republicans will raise such issues as citizen-initiated referenda.

The Swiss allow for popular initiatives, and have referenda on issues other than the constitution. Professor Galligan cites a study showing that Switzerland accounted for two-thirds of all of the world's referenda between 1945 and 1980. Australia came second!

The USA has adopted 25 amendments to their constitution. But the first 10, the Bill of Rights, were made in 1791 in order to secure ratification of the constitution itself. From 1791, there have only been 15. So Australia's eight changes in half the time do not seem as timid as critics suggest. Incidentally, American changes do not involve a referendum. Canada's constitution was amended 24 times before repatriation, but most of these were minor or technical changes.

Australia, because it has been so stable, has had little need to amend her constitution. Australians have resisted most changes giving Canberra more power, but high court interpretation of the constitution has in several important instances actually allowed this to occur.

As Brian Galligan says, the lack of formal changes is explained by the absence of revolution, conquest, military and political dictatorship and regionally based linguistic or ethnic communities, and the fact that the constitution was a fully democratic instrument of government from the start. (Gallagin, 120–122)

The power to alter the constitution was not, until 1986, exclusively contained in Section 128. (Of course, the high court, as the interpreter of the constitution, can also still effectively change the constitution. But this is not the place to enter into that engaging debate.) Until 1986, the power could also be exercised, in theory, by the imperial (British) parliament. However almost immediately after the constitution was enacted, it became an accepted convention that the imperial parliament would only legislate at the request of the relevant dominion. This convention can be seen in action when Western Australia voted by a referendum to secede and the petition was referred to London. After a careful examination it was pointed out that the Australian constitution contained its own formula for amendment. It was decided that the petition should have been referred to Canberra, not London.

The convention that the imperial power to legislate with respect to Australia should only be exercised at the request of

Australia was confirmed in the *Balfour Declaration* in 1926. This was incorporated into Section 4 of the *Statute of Westminster* 1931. And any residual power was terminated by the *Australia Acts* 1986 (s.1). How then can the *Statute of Westminster* or the *Australia Acts* be amended – as would need to be if a state wished to become a republic. The proposed law altering either or both *Westminster* or *Australia* can only be passed by the commonwealth parliament at the request or with the concurrence of the parliament of *all* the *states*. In other words all parliaments, state and federal, have to agree.

In preparation for the referendum on 6 November all states have passed legislation which will allow the commonwealth parliament to make such amendments necessary to allow a state to become a republic if it so wishes and if the referendum is carried. This was done without any public discussion or consultation.

THE STATES

The constitution is a schedule to the *Constitution Act*, an act of the British parliament. The preamble to this act (but not the constitution) recites that the people of each of the states "humbly relying on the blessing of Almighty God, have agreed to write in an indissoluble federal commonwealth under the crown . . ."

This British act could only be amended by the British parliament. After all it is a British act. The *Australia Act* 1986, passed by all of the Australian parliaments, and also by the British parliament, changes that. Now, if all of the state parliaments request, and the commonwealth parliament agrees, the commonwealth parliament can change the British act.

In one view, the effect of the *Australia Acts* is that not only must there be a successful referendum to create a republic, but also that all state parliaments must request the federal parliament to legislate to change the preamble before it can be changed by an act of the federal parliament. Some also argue that the people in *all* states – not just four – must agree to the referendum.

This view was rejected by the legal advisers to the Keating government's Republic Advisory Committee. They said that all that was required was a successful referendum approved as prescribed under s.128. Well, only the high court can decide this issue. Let me hasten to say that I am not suggesting we should challenge the holding of the referendum. I am merely observing that there could, at some stage, be a challenge to this process.

PLEBISCITES

It is important at this stage to distinguish between a referendum, as envisaged by the constitution, and a plebiscite. Plebiscites have been used, particularly in France, to manipulate the public into, for example, agreeing to make Napoleon Bonaparte and later his nephew, emperor and dictator. From the two Napoleons down to the recent attempt to take Quebec out of Canada, plebiscites are used for two purposes. First to deceive and mislead the people. Second, to obtain the constitutional equivalent of a blank cheque. From time to time we have heard suggestions that we have a plebiscite on the republican question. Paul Keating at one stage proposed a plebiscite with a question to this effect: "Are you in favour of the constitution being changed to provide for an Australian head of state?"

His proposed plebiscite was nothing more than a glorified opinion poll. It was obviously designed to get an affirmative vote, and to soften up voters and lock them in to the following referendum. Although Mr Keating's foray into plebiscites stalled, there have been incessant calls for one since.

The proposed questions vary but are designed to capture a maximum vote.

These proposed plebiscites reflect the series of opinion polls that various newspaper editors have commissioned over the years – not as impartial reporters of the facts, but as vigorous supporters of change. The opinion polls have been used for the same purpose as the proposed plebiscites. Just as a drip will eventually wear away the strongest stone, the opinion poll with the carefully designed question is used to wearing away resistance. Such an opinion poll is treated as "newsworthy" in itself. Now, is this not the most blatant manipulation of opinion? By publishing a series of polls, you have a subtle marketing exercise in inching the public towards the acceptance of the issues underlining the question. You can as a result insert into common parlance the arcane term "head of state". Then you can subtly suggest, through the words of the question, that the governor-general does not occupy this office of head of state. Or that the queen is "foreign". Or that Australia is not independent. If the question is repeated, and the results are splashed across the newspaper and picked up by the other media you begin to affect the debate.

In the meantime, other suggestions have been made about the use of plebiscites. For example, that an "indicative" plebiscite could be used allowing preferential voting between the present constitution and several republican models. The difficulty is that plebiscites have no legal effect – you still have to have a referendum. In such a plebiscite the people can be denied an informed vote. They will not get to see the details. The people deserve to be able to cast an informed vote. To do this they need to see what precisely is being proposed.

Constitutional plebiscites have been used in other countries to manipulate the public. When the Quebec government decided in 1995 it was time to secede from Canada, they knew they would need the support of the people in what was called a referendum, but in reality was a plebiscite.

The honest approach – the approach to ensure an informed vote – would have been to put all the facts before the Quebecois. In particular that there was no guarantee that even if Quebec were able to secede, the new state could retain the advantages it had enjoyed as part of Canada. Could Quebec continue to use the Canadian dollar? What would happen to the national debt? Would Quebec continue to be a party to each of Canada's treaties, for example the free trade treaty with the US and Mexico? Would Quebec's boundaries remain the same? And what of the indigenous people who preferred to stay in Canada. Could they secede from Quebec?

All of these unresolved issues were swept under the carpet. Instead, the referendum question was devised to attract a maximum vote. The aim was to have an uniformed vote.

This was the question that the Quebecois voted on: "Do you agree that Quebec should become sovereign, after having made a formal offer to Canada for a new economic and political partnership, within the scope of the bill respecting the future of Quebec and the agreement signed on 12 June 1995?"

To say the referendum question was misleading is an understatement. Exit polls demonstrated that many people who voted "yes" actually thought they were voting to stay in Canada. To the eternal credit of the Quebecois, they voted no. But only by a hairsbreadth. Because they were *not* properly informed. Now, Australians are no strangers to attempts to obfuscate the vote. Witness, for example, the recent 1998 referendum in the Northern Territory. Let us now look at what has actually happened in Australian referenda.

SUMMARY OF AUSTRALIAN REFERENDA

Since Federation, there have been 42 proposals to amend the constitution. Those 42 questions were put on 18 occasions. Only 13 of the 42 obtained a *national* majority. But of those 13, five were still unsuccessful. This was because three were approved in only three states and two were approved in only two states. To be successful they needed to have been approved in at least four states. So only eight of those 13 resulted in changes to the constitution.

There has been no case at all where a referendum has been approved in a majority of states, but has still failed to obtain a national majority. It is interesting to note that seven of the eight successful referenda were approved in *all* states. (The other one, in 1910, was approved in *five* states.) In fact, since 1910 *all* successful referenda have also been successful in *all* states.

It will be seen that of those referenda rejected, some were ill-advised economic measures that were also designed to concentrate more power in Canberra.

These were rejected not because of some recalcitrance, but because of the good sense of the Australian people. When it comes to their constitution, Australians undoubtedly take the conservative view which was enunciated by Lord Falkland in the English civil war: "When it is not necessary to change it is necessary not to change." It is hard to think of a better strategy when it comes to meddling in constitutional affairs.

The winning national percentages have ranged from as high as 90.77 per cent to as low as 54.39 per cent. The average is high, 73.525 per cent.

The eight successful referenda, with the national percentages in favour, were:

		per cent
1906	Senate elections	82.65
1910	State debts	54.95
1928	State debts	74.30
1946	Social services	54.39
1967	Aborigines	90.77
1977	Casual vacancies	73.32
1977	Retirement of Judges	80.10
1977	Territorial votes	77.72

The national percentage in those five unsuccessful referenda where only a national majority was obtained, were 53.56, 50.57, 50.30, 62.20, and 50.76 per cent respectively. These failed because they were approved in less than four states. Two were approved in only two states, three in three states. The only one of these five which came close to being passed was that on simultaneous elections in 1977. This obtained a national majority of 62.20 per cent, but only three states.

It is often said that a successful referendum needs the support of both government and opposition. But the 1967 referendum on the nexus between the senate and the house was supported by both and opposed by the small Democratic Labour Party. It was lost, gaining a national affirmative vote of only 40.25 per cent, and only winning in NSW.

Precedent suggests then that for a referendum proposal to be successful it not only requires the support of all the majority parties, it also needs widespread support *across* the Commonwealth. As a practical matter it needs to win *almost all* states and obtain a good national majority – at least 55 per cent, but more likely to be considerably higher. A referendum could theoretically succeed with 50.019 per cent votes nationally and majorities in four states. From experience, this seems most unlikely. Malcolm Turnbull has announced optimistically that two out of every three voters in New South Wales will vote Yes in the coming referendum. (*Daily Telegraph*, 11 December 1998) This seems unlikely. Australians are very cautious about constitutional change.

Crispin Hull, writing in the *Canberra Times*, on 2 January 1999, argues that the republic referendum is different because the republic will reduce the power of the prime minister. Members of the public will be able to nominate anyone and the choice will have to be approved by a two-thirds majority of parliament.

He skates over the fact that the prime minister can totally ignore the Presidential Nomination Committee's shortlist (most of whose members will be his) and the fact that the prime minister will be able to do what no other prime minister in any democracy can do – instantly and finally dismiss the constitutional umpire. Hull then gives a second reason. The republic corrects what has now become "a constitutional anachronism and is a blot on nationhood – having a person who lives in another country as Queen or King of Australia".

Is this the same constitutional anachronism and blot on nationhood that allows Canada, a proud NATO power, a member of the NAFTA group, to sit with the other six great western democracies in the exclusive G7?

Hull argues that previous precedents on failed referendums do not apply and he is not worried about the role of the real republicans who urge a No vote. He says: "Malcolm Turnbull has the convincing argument that an Australian head of state is a step towards that, rather than away from it, and a directly elected president would be easier to achieve from a position of having a president in the first place than from coming from scratch with a constitutional monarch."

A convincing argument? Wasn't this used for the Constitutional Convention when voters were told that the ARM's mind wasn't closed to direct election. It banged shut almost as soon as the convention began!

Hull concludes: "Surely, only the bog Irish would vote for the Queen."

REFERENDUM LAW AND PRACTICE

The referendum must be held between two and six months after the bill is passed by both houses. The main stages are that a bill setting out the proposed alteration to the constitution is passed by both houses of parliament; or if it is passed by one house only but rejected, fails to pass, or is altered in the other (and the alternations are unacceptable to the first house) and this is repeated in the next session of the parliament, the governor-general may put the proposal to the electors as last proposed by the first house with or without any amendments agreed by both houses.

Once passed by the parliament, the governor-general issues a writ for the referendum. The date set for the close of rolls is seven days after the issue of the writ. The polling day, which must be on a Saturday, is to be not less than 35 days or more than 58 days after the issue of the writ.

In 1912, s.6A was inserted into the *Referendum Act* to allow members and senators who voted for the bill, and those who voted against it, to prepare Yes and No cases for distribution. The electoral commissioner has the Yes and No cases printed together with a statement showing the proposed alterations. This must be posted to every elector on the roll no later than 14 days before polling day. (Between 1912 and 1928, parliament exempted certain referenda from this procedure.)

Voting procedures are similar to those for elections except that electors vote by writing either "Yes" or "No" in the box opposite each question on the ballot paper.

If the referendum obtains a double majority, the bill is then presented to the governor-general for the royal assent. There is no time limit prescribed for this.

REPEAT REFERENDA

In March 1999, Prime Minister John Howard had to remind republicans that there is no reason why a referendum can not be put more than once – if that is the wish of parliament or even of just one house. This was in response to a desperate argument that the referendum would be the "last chance" to vote on a republic.

Broadly speaking, the people have been asked to vote more than once on eight subjects. Three subjects have been submitted on two occasions – marketing schemes, freedom of religion and price control. Two subjects have been submitted on three occasions – trade and commerce and simultaneous elections. Three subjects have been submitted on five occasions – monopolies, corporations, and industrial matters.

Because a referendum question that failed has sometimes included more than one subject, it is difficult to know in each case which subject attracted the strongest opposition. The record for the greatest number of multiple subjects was the 1944 referendum on post-war reconstruction and democratic rights. It contained over twenty different subjects!

Some subjects just do not seem to appeal to the electorate. For example, price control and, strangely, freedom of religion. But to be fair, freedom of religion has never been put as a separate question.

Most of the failed referenda which involved giving more power to Canberra have been in many ways overtaken by high court decisions which have favoured the commonwealth.

Whenever a subject has been put again, it has failed to be approved. It is not true to say that if a question is put again, it always attracts a lower vote. Three repeat questions have come quite close to succeeding. Each gained *national* majorities but failed because only three states supported the referendum.

There is of course no reason why this record should be followed in the event of a second or subsequent republican referendum. And there is of course no guarantee that the referendum in November 1999 will fail. After all, it is supported by the Labor Party, most Democrats and many Liberal politicians. The broadsheet press is overwhelmingly favourable. The ARM is expected to be able to draw on the substantial resources of its leading supporters.

And if the 1998 Constitutional Convention elections are any indication, there will be no shortage of funds available to advertise the Yes case, in addition to the $7.5 million taxpayers' funds.

But if it fails, a subsequent republican referendum which is successful will break an Australian tradition.

While a good number of Australians will remain undecided until the campaign is underway, and those who argue the No case cannot be complacent, precedent suggests that Australians in all states will come to the referendum with their usual wisdom. And in this case, as the late Professor Patrick O'Brien said: "We are being asked by the nation's most famous and wealthiest former pig farmer to buy from him a pig-in-a-poke." (O'Brien, 40)

10

A MODEL CONSTITUTION

Real republicans, and most constitutionalists, recognise that no constitutional system is so perfect it should not change. What should be changed in ours?

There is a body of opinion that the status of the states has been subverted by centralist interpretations of the federal constitution.

Others draw attention to our voting systems, most of which can be changed by legislation.

The republican debate which the events of 1975, the ARM and Paul Keating unleashed has made us look at the very fundamental features of our Commonwealth of Australia.

When ACM Executive Director Kerry Jones and I appeared before the mainly republican commonwealth parliament Joint Select Committee on the Republic Referendum, one of the members expressed disinterest in any overseas examples of practice concerning governors-general. Fortunately, the founders of our constitution looked beyond the seas. If we are to re-examine the fundamental aspects of our constitutional system, we should do it so that we never again have to vote on a model hastily scrambled together just to secure the maximum votes at a convention. Whatever change is proposed should be based on sound constitutional principles.

There are, I suggest, only two international models of government worth considering. They are Westminster and Washington. We have to put aside Switzerland as a special case where a highly decentralised confederal structure allows for strong cantonal government, the co-existence of diverse linguistic groups, and such a wide use of citizen initiative referenda that the concept of representative government is significantly diluted.

Could we now go the way of the United States? There are significant differences between us, as there are between Canada and the USA. The crown founded Australia. Development was led by the crown. The USA was founded not so much by the crown but by dissident groups of people wishing to escape the religious rigours of the established church. They settled and developed their territories with a minimum role for government.

Nevertheless the American colonies still had the benefit of the laws, government of and defence forces of the mother country. All of this was done under an imperial umbrella. But even in their beginnings, they demonstrated a distance from the British crown that is in contrast to the Australian experience.

The thirteen American colonies were, before independence, the freest and most democratically governed colonies the world had ever seen.

So why did the Americans revolt? As British intellectual Paul Johnson argues, for once the characteristic British virtues of caution, pragmatism, practical common sense and moderation seemed to be absent in the ranks of those who governed in London. This, Johnson points out, would not have mattered much had the men who led America been men of ordinary stature. Unfortunately for Britain – and fortunately for America – the generation that emerged to lead the colonies into independence was "one of the most remarkable group of men in history – sensible, broad-minded, courageous, unusually well educated, gifted in a variety of ways, mature and long-sighted, sometimes lit by flashes of genius".

They were Enlightenment men "shorn of its vitiating French intellectual weaknesses of dogmatism, anti-clericalism, moral chaos and excessive trust in logic", and motivated by the English virtues of "pragmatism, fair mindedness, and honourable loyalty to each other".

The principle reason for revolt was taxation. Yet the American colonies were among the least taxed territories in recorded history. George Washington himself was an extremely rich man – who paid little tax. The British had doubled their national debt to pay for the Seven Year War, and the principal beneficiaries were the American colonies. These had a low public debt and paid on average one-fiftieth of the tax paid in the mother country. It seemed fair that the Americans contribute more.

The introduction of Grevilles *Stamp Act* to rectify this was the beginning of the end. The cry: "No taxation without representation" rallied opposition to London.

But while taxation was in the forefront, some of the other reasons for the revolt are less attractive. The British, having defeated the French, proposed to hand much of the land over to the traditional owners, the Native Americans, and to the settlers.

The *Great Proclamation* of 7 October 1773 by the British created a vast interior reserved for the Native Americans. Those settlers who had already crossed the boundary were ordered back. This gave justice to the indigenous people, but was a great error if the British wanted to keep the white settlers on side.

How many Australians, sympathising with the injustices borne by the Australian Aboriginal people, are aware of this skeleton in the American cupboard? The Native Americans were among the great losers from independence. And how many Australians are aware that once we received self-government, the moderating influence of the crown in protecting the Aborigines was lessened?

The other skeleton in the American closet was slavery. Although he was an abolitionist, John Adams had to omit any reference to abolition in the *Declaration of Independence*. In 1771, Lord Mansfield had held slavery to be unlawful in England under the common law. If a slave escaped to England, he was free: "The air of England is too pure for a slave to breathe." Without independence, could slavery have lasted long in the colonies? With independence, the number of slaves in the United States increased substantially.

The War of Independence was unpopular in Britain. Nor was

there unanimity among the Americans. Perhaps only one-third of Americans actually supported it. But British mismanagement, and an inability on their part to demonstrate traditional good sense, led to independence.

And what of American republicanism? Professor Graham Maddox argues that Machiavelli's influence on American republicanism was substantial. He says it was embraced by the American elite, its American lawyers and statesmen who, if not actually an "aristocracy", were certainly men of property, substance and learning – a true elite. And they owned slaves.

The founders were deeply conscious of their own talent and virtue. As Maddox says: "They had the opportunity to seize the American polity at the high point of their virtuous triumph over the corrupt forces of British imperialism. They tried to protect it against those future degenerations which, Machiavelli had taught, were in the end inevitable."

In taking Machiavelli's advice, they adopted a "mixed" constitution. While genuinely giving the people a say through the voting procedure, this was done in such a way that the influence of the people be neutralised. In the meantime, the real government would be conducted by an "aristocratic" element of elite elected representatives with a "monarchic", or rather consular, president. They entrenched their invention in a written instrument that could not be altered except by the most cumbersome process, and they established a Supreme Court to invalidate any "unconstitutional" acts of government.

There is no evidence that America is more democratic than Australia or better in protecting human rights. It is a more litigious, more violent and less caring society.

Perhaps the most obvious difficulty with the US constitution is that the impeachment of the president is such a process that government is paralysed and diverted for too long a time. During a recent crisis in supply in the United States, when the American embassy in Canberra closed down many of its functions, an exasperated American commented: "What we need is a governor-general!"

Would the separation of the legislature and the executive suit Australia? In the US, the president is extremely difficult to remove, and doesn't go when he should. The case of President Nixon is the best known example. Another incident just after President Kennedy's failed invasion of Cuba – the Bay of Pigs fiasco – is not so well known. The president explained to the Deputy Director of the CIA: "If this were the British government, I would resign and you, being a civil servant, would remain . . . But it isn't. In our government, you . . . have to go, and I have to remain." (*Spectator*, 24 June 1998)

What of other countries?

Most of the continental constitutions are relatively new. Those of unitary states such as Ireland are not a good model for Australia. By making the Irish president powerless, the prime minister's powers are increased. This may work in a unitary state that has long enjoyed the financial benefits of the European Union. It would not work in Australia. Even the Republic Advisory Committee chaired by Malcolm Turnbull agreed about this. Australia, unlike EU countries, can't look to massive financial transfers from other states, or protected internal trade, as Ireland has enjoyed. We are more on our own.

The constitutions of the former Axis powers, Germany, Italy and Japan were designed to prevent a repetition of their fascist post, but have not yet been tested in a crisis. They are hardly suitable models.

What of France, from which both revolution and the continental forms of modern republicanism come? Surely France could provide a model for Australian republicans?

In fact the French know more about constitutional models than most countries. France has experienced an absolute then a constitutional monarchy, five republics, a restored monarchy, then a "bourgeois monarchy", two empires, various revolutionary regimes (Legislative Assembly, Convention, Directorate, Consulate) as well as the Vichy dictatorship. Incidentally, all of this occurred in France in the time that Australia evolved from a penal colony to autonomy, to federation and to independence. We should never forget that we are more experienced in democratic government than any of the principal mainland European powers, indeed any major world power except the United Kingdom, the United States and Canada.

The First French Republic ended in the Reign of Terror and then Bonaparte's dictatorship which he converted into the First Empire. The Second Republic was converted, through the use or rather the abuse of the plebiscite, into the dictatorship of the Second Empire.

The Third Republic provides some interesting case studies on presidents chosen by parliament.

Under the Third Republic (1871–1940), the president was elected not by the people but by the National Assembly. The understanding was that he was to reign, and not to rule. The first president, Adolphe Thiers, resigned in 1873 within two years of his election when his preferred government lost a vote of confidence in parliament. He expected to be recalled and had planned to restore his party to office. He was mistaken. He was succeeded by Marshal Patrice de McMahon, who in 1877 used his reserve powers to dismiss the government. He argued that while the prime minister was responsible to parliament, he, as president, was responsible to France. When his party was not returned to government, he resigned. The third president, Jules Grévy (1879–1887), was noted for using all his power and influence in the election of the prime minister. He regarded foreign affairs and military matters as his own "domaine reservé". He played a major role in Franco-German relations but he resigned after his brother-in-law was convicted for selling favours, including honours. Another president, Jean Casimir-Perier, was so provocatively authoritarian in his inaugural address that this unleashed a campaign for his removal. Fortunately he resigned within five months of his election in 1895.

Some presidents of the Third Republic are remembered more for the way they died than for what they did during their terms.

When the unfortunate Paul Doumer was elected in 1931 by 504 votes out of 883 he said, inexplicably: "With votes like these,

I'll only be assassinated." He was when opening a book exhibition in the Maison Rothschild. His assistants, wishing to spare his feelings, told him he had been knocked down by a taxi! His last words, "Quel chauffeur!" (What a driver!) were understandable. He no doubt wondered what a taxi was doing in the Maison Rothschild.

Felix Faure (1895–1899) also regarded foreign affairs as his, and played a major role in cementing the Franco-Russian Alliance. He refused to reopen the Dreyfus case, an infamous example of injustice and anti-Semitism. One of the peculiar arguments of the ARM is that the politician's president who emerges from their republic will somehow be a focus for the unity of the nation. If presidents can unify a country, Felix Faure unified France more in his passing than anything he did in his life. This occurred in the course of what the French describe as a "rendezvous gallant" with Mme Stenheil, whose cries caused staff to burst in to release her hair from the deceased president's hands. He is celebrated by an avenue in Paris, and countless other avenues and Rues Felix Faure throughout France.

His successor, Emile Loubet (1899–1906), also claimed a special role in foreign affairs. (Isn't one of the arguments for an Australian president that he or she can represent us in other countries? We shall then have two foreign ministers, or three if we count the prime minister. Or will this be a "domaine reservé" for our president?) Not all presidents of the Third Republic thought they should rule. Armand Fallieres (1906–1913) was one who behaved impeccably, as if he were a constitutional monarch. He seems to have been in a minority.

If the French experience shows anything, it is that politicians are no better, and probably worse, at selecting presidents than the people.

When the National Assembly elected Paul Deschanel in 1920, his opponent Clemenceau exclaimed, "But they've elected a madman!" Unfortunately, Clemenceau was right and parliament was wrong. At Nice, after a speech was well received with cries of "Bis" (encore), Deschanel gave it again, in full! On his way to

Montbrison, he fell out of the presidential train and was found wandering along the trace in his pyjamas. The music halls resounded with a new song "Le Pyjama Presidentiel". After seven months, he was persuaded to resign. He was succeeded in 1920 by Alexandre Millerand, who shocked even the French by his blatant intervention in government. He forced the foreign minister, Aristide Briand, to resign. He even campaigned for the Bloc National in the legislative elections. But unlike President Deschanel, he lasted until 1924.

The last president of the third republic, Albert Lebrun, to his credit, refused to resign in 1940 to allow Marshal Petain to be appointed dictator. Another deal, another trade-off? Petain was appointed anyway, and three days later Lebrun did resign. Nobody noticed. The new Vichy regime was more eager than even the Nazis expected in deporting Jews to Germany. Charles de Gaulle was condemned to death in *absentia*. Who put this appalling regime in power? Not the *people* of France. It was the *parliament* who chose the president.

The next republic, the fourth, had a parliamentary elected president. It did not last long. It was born in Algiers with a Provisional Government (GPRF) under General Charles de Gaulle in 1943. Its death rattles began, again in Algiers, when the former governor-general of Algeria, Jacques Soustelle, attempted a coup d'état. The last president, Reny Coty, threatened to resign unless de Gaulle was recalled and the parliament granted him supreme powers. Which they did. Unlike Petain, de Gaulle introduced a new constitution that retained democratic elections.

The Fifth Republic was born in 1959 and de Gaulle was chosen president by an Electoral College. He too was expected to reign rather than rule. But he then gave a new constitution what one commentator describes as a "presidentialiste" interpretation. In particular, he regarded foreign affairs as his "domaine reservé". To everyone's surprise, he failed to confirm Georges Pompidou as prime minister after Pompidou won a landslide victory after the student uprising in 1968. When de Gaulle resigned in 1969, Pompidou succeeded him.

I recall not so long ago the French news broadcast in Australia by SBS opening with an announcement by President Chirac dissolving the National Assembly. He needed no advice to do this. And the president is treated with un-Australian deference on television. It is as if he were a king, but a political king.

None of the French regimes has lasted the time of our Australian system. None of the French Republics is in any way superior to, or as good as, the Australian system.

So could we graft a republic onto the Westminster system? The result is *always* inferior. Why? Because it creates another political office occupied by a politician.

This is reason why we do not elect our judges. They would become too political.

The Westminster system is headed by the *dignified* part of the constitution, the crown acting through the governor-general, and the governors. These are non-political offices, important in a unitary state but essential in a Westminster federation such as Australia. The crown must therefore arbitrate and audit, especially but not only between the people's house and the state's house.

Westminster began and works best with a constitutional monarch. Grafting a president onto Westminster will always resulted in an inferior system. Westminster republics do not work as well in crises – the French Third and Fourth Republics and the Italian republic are examples. The Indian Republic seems to work quite well, but it is marred by the politicisation of the offices of the president and especially the state governors, who are appointed by Delhi, not by the state governments. Certainly before independence, the viceroy and the governors were instruments of imperial policy, but outside of that, they had begun to play the important role of umpire and auditor as home government developed.

The worst constitutional crisis was during the government of Indira Ghandi.

In seeing her fortunes falling and fearing prosecution for alleged crimes, India's Prime Minister Indira Ghandi decided to declare a state of emergency. This would in effect sweep aside all democratic constraints on the government. She would enjoy dictatorial powers. Obviously this regime was intended for genuine emergencies. There was one catch. The declaration had to be signed by the president. When she put it under his nose, he hesitated. Where was the emergency? As far as he could see there was none.

She reminded him sharply that she and the Congress Party had put him into office. He was *their* man. He signed.

In 1901 Australia's founders knew there were only two possible models which could be applied to Australia: the Westminster system – preferably bi-cameral with an independent head of state to ensure legality and to balance the "elected dictatorship" that results from government control of the lower house; or the American model, where the executive is also the head of state and is separate from the legislature.

After 100 years we now know something the founders did not. In this century we have seen the widespread export of four constitutional systems. The first two were the most horrific failures. These constitutional systems either were never democratic, or if they were, allowed dangerous concentrations of power to develop. And inevitably, to be abused. They are not worthy of further comment apart from noting them: the Fascist system from Italy and Germany, and Soviet Communism from Russia. They have been consigned to where they belong – the rubbish dump of history.

The other two are Westminster, from Britain, and the US system. For those who are looking for a model republic to import, there is one fact to bear in mind. Of the world's seven great long lasting democracies, five follow the Westminster system. All five are monarchies. The Westminster system, when exported, can work very well.

The others are Switzerland and the US. No one follows Switzerland, for reasons we have discussed. Many countries have adopted the US system, especially in Latin America. One was a country which in 1901 compared to Australia in economic terms – Argentina. All have ended in upheaval, coups, revolutions and military government. Was this a coincidence? The question is whether the Washington model is exportable. The historical fact is that *only* the Westminster system has been successfully exported.

This is not to say there cannot be reforms to other aspects of the Australian constitutional system. Australia has demonstrated this both by its innovations, for instance the secret ballot, and its adapted imports, for instance the referendum. Other changes can be debated and if the people agree, can be introduced. Indeed, if the November 1999 referendum is lost, real republicans may well seek to emphasise reforms to other aspects of our constitutional arrangements.

In the meantime, when we ponder the Keating–Turnbull republic, it would be difficult not to agree that the onus on those seeking fundamental change is heavy. As it ought to be. In all the debates, the case put by the ARM has been found wanting. They have not satisfied – they have not even come close – to satisfying the onus of proof.

11
FLAGGING THE REPUBLIC

If a republic is about symbols, what of our chief national symbol, the Australian National Flag?

The origins of Australia's National Flag go back to just before Federation in 1900, when the Melbourne newspaper the *Evening Herald* and then the *Review of Reviews for Australasia*, sponsored national flag competitions. On 29 April 1901, the new commonwealth government announced its own competition for the design of a national flag.

It then was agreed to combine the *Review of Reviews* competition with the commonwealth government's, with a total prize of two hundred pounds, a substantial sum in those days. Designs submitted to the *Herald*'s competition were also considered. The judges were to have been the six premiers, but they were replaced by seven men with appropriate qualifications. By the closing date 32,823 entries had been received. The prize was divided between five contestants who submitted similar designs. Two were teenagers. One, Ivor Evans, was only 14.

The government accepted the judges' advice. The *Commonwealth Government Gazette* of 20 February 1903 noted that the King had approved the *Flag of the Commonwealth of Australia*, a blue ensign, as the *Blue Ensign of the Commonwealth*, and a red ensign as the merchant flag.

It is often claimed by those who want to impose some new flag on Australians that one condition of the competition was that all designs be "based on the British Ensign" and thus incorporate the British union flag, the "Union Jack". Mr E.J. Eggins, the Honorary Secretary of the Australian National Flag Association – a voluntary community service organisation – has laboured long to inform Australians about the importance and significance of Australians' chief national symbol. (Much of the historical information in this chapter comes from the Association.) He has exposed this claim to be baseless. (*Sydney Morning Herald*, 3 February 1999) The conditions were set out in the *Commonwealth Government Gazette*, 29 April 1901. There were in fact *no* conditions limiting the design.

In 1908, the government announced a minor change to the flag. A seven-pointed star, symbolic of the six states and territories, would replace the original large six-pointed star. (*Commonwealth Government Gazette*, 19 December 1908) The Southern Cross of course relates to our geographic location, and the crosses on the union flag represent the principles on which our nation is based – parliamentary democracy, the rule of law and freedom of speech. In 1957, King George VI approved a recommendation that the commonwealth blue ensign be adopted as the Australian Flag. By the *Flag Act*, 1953, which had the strong support of both sides of the parliament, the commonwealth blue ensign was declared to be the *Australian National Flag*, and the red ensign the *Australian Red Ensign*.

In more recent years, the organisation Ausflag has campaigned vigorously for a new flag, or rather – to get rid of the Australian National Flag. This movement was given considerable exposure when Paul Keating was prime minister in the years 1993–96.

Ausflag ran a national flag design competition in 1997–98. Among its sponsors were two multinational corporations, one Japanese and one American. This reliance on foreign support attracted considerable criticism. But as with the republic, getting rid of our existing symbols and institutions is seen as more important than any resulting division in the community. One hundred flags, described as the finalists, were featured in colour on a full page of the *Sydney Morning Herald* on 26 January 1998. That this was Australia Day, and would be seen as highly provocative, apparently disturbed neither the organisers nor the editor. Readers were invited to vote by telephone. And in the bottom right hand corner was the present Australian National Flag. An editorial the next day talked of the inevitability of change. It said Ausflag had "compelling evidence" that Prime Minister Menzies had changed the Australian Flag in 1953 from red to blue because red had connotations of communism! (Presumably, the Labor leader, Evatt must have agreed, as he also strongly supported the legislation.)

The president of the Australian National Flag Association, John Vaughan, replied that while the editor might believe Ausflag's evidence to be compelling but ... in fact, approval of the blue Australian flag, and the Australian Red Ensign as our merchant flag was officially proclaimed in the *Commonwealth Government Gazette* of 20 February 1903. "It is noted with regret that the *Herald* has become an active promoter of the anti-Australian flag agenda of Ausflag Ltd." (*Sydney Morning Herald*, letters, 6 February 1998)

Notwithstanding this evidence, it is sometimes claimed by prominent republicans that the first time Australians served under the blue ensign was in Vietnam.

The result of the competition must have been disappointing for Ausflag. The Australian National Flag received 8253 votes, for the second choice only 1581.

In the following year, 1999, the *Sydney Morning Herald* publicised another competition, featuring three flags and the Australian National Flag. One of the three was the separate winner of what was described as the Ausflag "People's Choice" competition. And still the Australian National Flag won the poll.

In the meantime, various emblems were being changed or removed throughout the country – a form of republicanism by stealth. Because it was feared a subsequent government might change the flag without consulting the people, some argued that the flag should be entrenched in the constitution.

When Ausflag said this could not or should not be done, as a matter of principle, a letter from the author was published in the

Sydney Morning Herald pointing out the tri-colour was in fact entrenched in the French constitution. In any event a new government, led by John Howard, introduced a bill to amend the *Flag Act*. This became law in 1998. It provides that the Australian National Flag can only be changed after a majority of electors, voting at a plebiscite in which the Australian National Flag is included, choose a new flag.

Although the act could presumably by repealed or even challenged, only a foolhardy government would try to change the Australian National Flag without the consent of the people.

The ARM argues that the 1999 referendum on the republic has nothing to do with changing the flag. But as former governor-general Bill Hayden argues, if the Keating–Turnbull republic is adopted, the same "small group of activists" will then target the flag. Paul Keating chose not to fly the Australian flag on his car when he was prime minister. And Kim Beazley indicated the Keating government was working towards changing the flag around 2001 for the Centenary of Federation. (*Daily Telegraph Mirror*, 6 June 1994)

Notwithstanding ARM protestations that the referendum has nothing to do with changing the flag, it seems to be ready to lend support for change. Perhaps the most startling occasion was the exhibition "Flagging the Republic" at Sydney's Sherman Galleries Goodhope, in association with the New England Regional Art Museum. According to the catalogue, the exhibition was supported by the Australian Republican Movement. The following appeared in a large endorsement under its logo and name:

The Australian Republican Movement is dedicated to the achievement of a republic in Australia, with an Australian as our head of state, by 1 January 2001. In promoting images of Australia the artists in this exhibition are demonstrating a commitment to Australia. It is that commitment we share in supporting this exhibition.

The program also states that the exhibition is "sponsored" by, among others, Turnbull & Partners Limited, Investment Bankers–

ARM leader Malcolm Turnbull's company. Ausflag's role is also acknowledged.

The seventy flags in the exhibition did not of course include the Australian National Flag. There is one with a cockatoo's head occupying half the flag, and stripes on the remainder. Appropriate perhaps for a beach towel, hardly one for the national symbol. But the most surprising was a flag with a white background, on which is printed in large letters "F*** OFF BACK TO FAGLAND". "Fagland" presumably is derived from the word "fag", a pejorative term from the United States for a homosexual. "Fagland" is apparently intended to mean the United Kingdom.

Had any organisation on the other side of this debate been involved in this it would have been the object of a vast and continuing exposé in the media, and complaints to the authorities. There would have been denunciations in parliament and in the press.

Some very careful discreet reporting ensured that the ARM and the sponsors were saved from embarrassment and outrage.

The fact is that neither this "flag", nor any of the others has commanded any significant support as a replacement.

It is apparent that, with some individual exceptions, the same broad coalition of elite interests who wish to impose the Keating–Turnbull republic also want to get rid of our national flag. It will be the next target. Obviously success in this referendum will give a platform to change the Australian National Flag, the symbol of the Australia most Australians cherish.

12
THE STATES

The view of the proponents of both Keating–Turnbull republics is that it is possible to remove the crown from the federal constitution, but for the states to remain monarchies. The reason for this approach can only be expedience, not principle.

The attorney-general, Darryl Williams QC, has described piecemeal change as "a constitutional monstrosity". As Sir Anthony Mason – a republican – asked at a seminar on 11 May 1998 at the Australian National Museum, "Why we should amend the constitution to enable such a monstrosity to be thrust on us is not easy to understand." The reason is that the ARM, and the other official republicans, are so desperate for change that they are not prepared to do it properly.

Apart from the process of change, the second Keating–Turnbull republic proposes a significant reduction in the role and influence of the states, in particular the smaller states. The appointment of a single candidate as the president will be by a joint sitting of the two houses, where the more populous state will dominate. But it is in the dismissal of the president that the power of the states' house, the senate, is totally removed.

The only consequence of dismissal is a vote in the house of representatives within 30 days, which was to be treated as a vote of confidence in the government, although the bill for the referendum does not say this. Even if the vote were lost, which is unlikely, the president would not be restored to office. He would be re-eligible to be considered as a candidate, but how likely would it be the prime minister would choose him again? In addition the prime minister can ensure that he has his person in place either by keeping a compliant president in office beyond his term, or ensuring his agent acts as president. Not only does the senate have absolutely no role in the dismissal of the president, the senate's powers over supply will have been completely neutralised. So for the first time in centuries, a Westminster government will be able to rule without supply, thus reversing a fundamental principle of constitutional law.

This republic runs counter to the generally accepted principles of our system of government. Two are relevant here. First there will be a serious diminution in the power and authority of the senate. Second it opens up the possibility of a government ruling without supply, which is contrary to all accepted constitutional principles. Is this the revenge and the "cure" for 1975?

THE PROPER PROCESS FOR CHANGE

Rushing into a republic through a federal referendum, perhaps only with the barest of majorities and only in four states, is not the way to proceed. Why do we need to hurry? If it is at the instigation of those so obsessed by the millennium and the Olympic Games that they demand constitutional change, they are precisely the sort of people who should not be allowed near the constitution.

The process is extremely complex. There are serious legal doubts (too complex to detail here) about the ways the various legal provisions interlock under our constitutions, state and federal, the *Statute of Westminster* and the *Australia Acts*. As republican and former Chief Justice Sir Anthony Mason argued at a seminar at Parliament House in Sydney on 27 May 1998, an agreement between the commonwealth and the states as to the steps to implement a republic would have been desirable. It would be a pity, he said, if the move were to "degenerate into a series of legal controversies to be determined by the courts".

Any move to a republic should surely reflect the movement to federation. It was the *people* in each of the six states who agreed to form an indissoluble federal commonwealth under the crown. To change the fundamental aspects of this compact, a new compact is necessary. This should have begun with an agreement between the states and the commonwealth, ratified by all parliaments. This then could have been put at simultaneous federal and state referenda. Although this may not be strictly necessary in every state, it is inconceivable that such a change would be attempted in any state without a referendum.

The agreement could also provide for appropriate changes to the other constitutional laws, the *Statute of Westminster* and the *Australia Acts*. The difficulty with this process is that there would need to have emerged a consensus for change first, at least as strong as that in the late nineteenth century. That sadly is not the process which has been chosen. The ARM was given the opportunity – a most generous opportunity – to come up with a model that would command the necessary widespread support. But as Professor Geoffrey Blainey has observed, while it was easy during the Keating years for the ARM to be destructive, when it came to being constructive, the ARM failed the test dismally. The second Keating–Turnbull republic was the result of deals and "back of the envelope" drafting, even on the floor of the convention. It even failed to command a majority there.

There are two possible conclusions. The first is that a patient consultative process will produce a model which has the widespread support to pass through the process I have described – federal and state. Bills for simultaneous referenda would all need to be passed. The second is that it is not possible to devise such a model, at least a model that is as good as the existing one.

If the referendum fails on 6 November 1999 only time will tell which conclusion is correct.

NEW ZEALAND

It is proposed to delete New Zealand from the definition of a "state". Although New Zealand clearly does not wish at the present time to become part of the Commonwealth of Australia, and this is unlikely to change in the foreseeable future, it would be unwise to make it difficult for this to occur should circumstances change. Unless the original definition is retained, the possibility of New Zealand entering the commonwealth under the existing constitution would be precluded. We have left the door open for about 100 years.

Why close it now?

THE INDIVISIBILITY OF THE AUSTRALIAN CROWN

Until the delivery in 1993 to the Keating government of the Republic Advisory Committee Report, no one seriously argued that the crown of Australia could be anything but one and indivisible. This flows from the *indissolubility* of the Federal Commonwealth of Australia. There were not separate state crowns. When the government of NSW acts, it is the crown of Australia in the right of New South Wales – not the crown of New South Wales. This distinction is not just semantic. A separate crown of New South Wales, Queensland or Western Australia would suggest that each could develop into a separate country, as Australia did from the British Empire.

When Australia became independent, the states had wished to retain a certain independence from Canberra in their relations with the sovereign. When the convention developed that the governor-general was appointed on the advice of the Australian prime minister, the states did not wish to see the governor-general become a viceroy. If he had it would have been governor-general who would have appointed the governors on the advice of the prime minister, not the sovereign. This is the Canadian practice, where the lieutenant-governors are appointed by the governor-general. Taken a stage further in republican India, the governors are appointed by the president and they represent very clearly the interests of the central government.

So the practice remained of the state governments advising the British government of their preference for appointment as governor, and the British government so advising the queen. This was a pragmatic and sensible solution that escaped the attention of the chattering classes for some time.

When Gough Whitlam was prime minister, he proposed that this anomaly, as he saw it, should cease. Only the prime minister should advise the crown on the appointment of the state governors. State premiers would not longer advise the queen through the British government. The state premiers rose in unison against this, and the plan to make the governor-general a viceroy failed.

Later Sir Colin Hannah, the Governor of Queensland, inadvisably criticised the record of the Whitlam government. On Gough Whitlam's recommendation the "dormant" commission governors usually hold to act as administrator of the commonwealth in the absence of the governor-general was removed from Sir Colin.

It was reported that subsequently a Labor Party representative requested the British Labor government not to recommend Sir Colin's re-appointment as governor to the queen if the Queensland government were to propose it. The Callaghan government apparently accepted this advice, and let the Queensland government know that a recommendation to reappoint Sir Colin would be unacceptable.

The weakness of the use of the British government as an envoy was thus exposed. But the British government was well used to the problem of its involvement in federal realms, particularly with Canada.

A solution was found in the *Australia Acts* 1986. These ensured the continuing independence of the states in the choice of their governors. It is said that this was initially opposed by Canberra and that palace advisers were also opposed to the premiers being able to advise the queen directly. This was adopted only after the direct intervention of the queen. This procedure ensures the governors would not become "prefects" in the service of the federal government. The process entrenched in the *Australia Acts*, and could only be changed by the Australian parliament acting on the request or approval of all state parliaments.

THE HEPTARCHY – A CONSTITUTIONAL MONSTROSITY!

The Republican Advisory Committee established by the Keating government concluded that both state and federal constitutions could be changed by one referendum. To be successful, they said, it would only need a national majority of those voting and a majority in four states. The authority for this is said to be section 15(3) of the *Australia Acts*. But this merely preserves, but does not extend the use to which a referendum may be put under our constitution.

Under the *Republic Bill* it was originally intended to override the veto of each state. Under proposed clause 7 of proposed schedule 2 to the constitution, the commonwealth parliament was to be given the power to amend section 7 of the *Australia Acts*, at the request of one state only, and only as regards that state. This was of doubtful validity as the scheme established by those acts clearly requires all states to request the commonwealth to take this action. Clause 7 in fact became unnecessary as all states adopted legislation requesting the commonwealth to act if the referendum were passed. It was withdrawn in the last days before the *Republic Bill* was passed. The point to note is that there was a willingness to override the *Australia Acts* scheme giving each state a veto. This is indicative of readiness to concentrate power in Canberra, which is a feature of the Keating–Turnbull republic.

In any event, one may wonder why section 15 of the *Australia Acts* granted each state parliament a veto over such a change if it can be so easily undermined. That hardly seems likely. Knowing that such a referendum would be seen as provocative and heavy-handed, and this less likely to be approved by the people, the Republic Advisory Committee chose to recommend against the total abolition of the crown.

In other words, the proponents of the Keating–Turnbull republic only refrained from forcing the states to convert to republics along with the federation for fear that such a referendum would be easier to defeat.

The states in a future federal republic are obviously to be made much more subject to central control.

To give legal support for this piecemeal change, the RAC "discovered" that rather than being one monarchy Australia was in fact seven monarchies. A "heptarchy"! This is a pure invention. Until then there was a consensus that Australia was a single federal entity – an "indissoluble federal commonwealth under the crown".

It is possible for separate monarchical and republican states to agree to federate into a large entity. This was the case in Germany until 1919, where the republican city-states of Bremen, Hamburg and Lübeck united with several monarchies into an empire under the Kaiser, and until 1857, one Swiss canton was a monarchy, Neuchâtel.

But what is being proposed in Australia is entirely different. That is that the single indivisible crown of Australia, which dates at least from 1931, and is the crown of this indissoluble federal commonwealth, should in 1999 or 2000 become eight crowns, one of which should then disappear.

The division of the old imperial crown into several occurred to give legal effect to the independence of Canada, Australia, Newfoundland, South Africa, New Zealand and the Irish Free State. The decision of the Australian crown could in law have a similar result.

As the distinguished constitutional lawyer, Robert Elliott QC, said in August 1999: "If the republic referendum were passed, it could split the Federation."

West Australian Premier Richard Court warned the Constitutional Convention of the consequences of the change proposed: "At worst, the states not wanting to become a republic could secede from the Federation. At best, each state would have to rewrite its own constitution."

If there is to be a crown of Queensland or Western Australia the commonwealth is now dissoluble. This is saying that South Australia or Tasmania or any state is free to decide its future. *The Constitution Alteration (Establishment of Republic)*, 1999 – the Referendum Bill – attempts to counter this in clause 6 of the transitional provisions. This purports to ensure the continuity of the federal system. But if this is already dissolved by the piecemeal approach, is it effective?

Ignoring constitutional theory and practice, the ARM and its allies are prepared to risk the unity of the nation. Not by design, I hasten to add, but because of this unhealthy obsession with getting rid of the queen at any price.

13
THE COMMONWEALTH OF NATIONS

The transition of the old British Empire into the Commonwealth of Nations has been one of the most remarkable developments of this century. No other empire before, or since, has voluntarily handed over the reins of government to its colonies. There was an attempt in the 1980s to create a similar organisation between the republics of the former Soviet Union. The word "commonwealth" was even used. The attempt failed.

The British had learned from those mistakes which had led to the war of independence with the United States. Yet before independence, the British colonies there were the most free, and the most autonomous, that the world had yet seen.

It is sometimes forgotten today that in the middle of the last century, Britain enjoyed responsible government, liberal institutions and the rule of law, as well as considerable personal freedom. As Bogdanor observes, these elements were readily transferred to the settler colonies in Canada, Australia, New Zealand and parts of South Africa. The mainland European empires did not and could not do this. Why? Because they did not themselves enjoy such benefits in their home countries!

The great impetus to decolonisation was the *Durham Report* of 1839. Recognising that the Canadian provinces already had their own representative legislatures, Lord Durham proposed a further, even more radical step. This was that the government of those provinces, through the sovereign's viceregal representatives, would no longer be responsible to London. He recommended that part of government in respect of domestic affairs be conducted still by the crown, but the crown acting on the advice of ministers responsible to the colonial legislature. Not the crown acting on the advice of the British ministers. There we see the beginning of a separate Canadian crown.

At one stroke the main tension between the colonies and London was removed. The evolutionary move to independence in Canada, Australia and New Zealand received a remarkable stimulus. It had its origins in the fact that the rule of law, and all its benefits, came with the settlers of each new colony at its very foundation. It was in Adelaide in 1884 that Lord Rosebery, later the British prime minister, described this trend accurately by stating that the Empire was now a Commonwealth of Nations.

In the latter part of the nineteenth century it was even recognised that the colonial governments had some limited right to deal with foreign powers. A half-hearted move to develop an imperial federation went against this trend. It commanded little support. By 1917, at the Imperial War Conference, it was formally agreed that a readjustment of the constitutional relations in the Empire should be made based on a full recognition of the dominions (as the self-governing colonies came to be called) as "autonomous nations of an Imperial Commonwealth". At the Versailles Conference at the end of the First World War Australia (and the other dominions) signed the *Treaty of Versailles*, and became a full founding member of the League of Nations. In 1920 Canada and the United States entered into full and separate diplomatic relations with one another. In 1923 the unfettered right of the dominions to enter into treaties was confirmed. Unlike the British, the dominions did not sign the *Treaty of Lausanne* with Turkey in 1923. And the substantial obligations Britain agreed to in Europe under the *Treaty of Locarno* in 1925 did not extend to the dominions.

These developments were not initiated by, but were recognised in, the celebrated *Balfour Declaration* of 1926, which affirmed that the dominions were "autonomous communities within the British Empire, equal in status, in no way subordinate to one another in any respect of their domestic or internal affairs, though united by a common allegiance to the crown and associated as members of the British Commonwealth of Nations". And from 1930, governors-general were to be appointed by the sovereign on the advice of the dominion government. They were to continue in their principal role as the constitutional umpire and auditor in the dominion. They had in 1926 already lost their other subordinate role as representatives of the imperial government. This was to go to the high commissioners, who would represent commonwealth governments in other capitals.

The change flowed from an earlier decision in 1926 that a governor-general holds "in all essential respects, the same position in relation to the administration of public affairs" in the dominion concerned "as is held by His Majesty the King in Great Britain, and that he is not the representative or agent" of the British government.

In 1930, the first Australian governor-general, Sir Isaac Isaacs, was appointed on the advice, indeed at the insistence, of the Australian prime minister. The King had earlier suggested that there was an advantage in having a governor-general who had no connections with the local political scene, and who was already personally known to him.

When Britain declared war on Germany in 1939, the reaction of the dominions was not uniform. Eire (now the Republic of Ireland) decided on neutrality. Canada and later South Africa declared war. The Australian prime minister, R.G. Menzies, in announcing the declaration by Britain, declared that "as a result, Australia is at war".

It was becoming clear that the old concept of a single indivisible imperial crown was no longer tenable. There were now several crowns. And in 1937 Ireland (Eire) became, or became close to being, a republic, a fact accepted by the other members.

In 1942, the British government accepted that an independent India could secede from the commonwealth. Burma did so in 1947, as Ireland did in 1948, first securing a treaty with Britain that confirmed the special relationship between them.

In 1947, when India became independent, she indicated she wished to become a republic but to stay within the commonwealth. It had long been clear – at least to those with vision – that independence would in due course be granted to the other colonies in Asia, Africa, and the West Indies. For there was no reason why other people should not enjoy the same rights that for example, Australians and Europeans enjoyed. The imperial authorities had already recognised the inherent equality of the races of the Empire. For instance, in 1856 the British had insisted on a common role of voters – not one based on race – in their colony in South Africa. The Colonial Secretary had declared in 1897 that the imperial tradition made "no distinction in favour of, or against race or colour".

This liberal tradition sometimes ran counter to the views of the white populations in the settled colonies. This was particularly true of Australia, where responsible governments frequently adopted policies in relation to both the indigenous people and to immigration that caused tensions with governors and colonial secretaries. This aspect of our history is often forgotten, perhaps conveniently so.

In 1947 the commonwealth could have rejected India. But this was likely to have led to the exclusion of many, if not all, of the new commonwealth countries that might wish to follow India. In other words, the commonwealth would have become principally a white man's club. So that all of the members agreed that India could continue as a member, even as a republic. This procedure is now followed whenever a realm wishes to become a republic. India formally did accept "the King as the symbol of the free association of its independent member state and as such the head of the Commonwealth". And on the death of George V, his daughter, Elizabeth II, was by common consent, proclaimed "Head of the Commonwealth".

All of the old dominions, with the exception of South Africa, have remained in the commonwealth as realms, with Elizabeth II as queen, and so have twelve other former colonies. These, with the UK, number sixteen. Six member states share national monarchies: Brunei, Lesotho, Malaysia, Swaziland, Tonga and Western Samoa. The remainder – all "new" commonwealth states – are republics.

All parties to the republican debate in Australia have indicated their wish that whatever the outcome of the referendum, Australia should remain a member of the commonwealth. Indeed, the ARM has consistently stated, without qualification, that if Australia becomes a republic, she *will* continue a member of the commonwealth. And the Australians for Constitutional Monarchy has just as consistently pointed to the actual practice that the consent of all other members of the commonwealth is necessary.

In May 1999 Attorney-General Daryl Williams repeated the ARM view during a speech:

The Australian Government proposes that the name, Commonwealth of Australia, be retained and that Australia continue to be a member of the Commonwealth of Nations. Australia would not need to reapply for membership of the Commonwealth if it becomes a republic as constitutional status is not a criterion of membership.

This would mean that if the proposed change were supported Australia would still participate in the Commonwealth Games. (*Canberra Times*, Monday, 10 May 1999)

ACM believed this statement could not go uncorrected. It was part of a wider message – that the change was only symbolic, and was quite simple. So as ACM National Convenor I stated that, were Australia to become a republic, any of the other 53 commonwealth governments might be able to block its continuing membership of the commonwealth.

I pointed out that in 1960 South Africa withdrew after it became a republic, accepting that not all of the other governments would consent to its continuing membership. And Fiji's membership was deemed to lapse in 1987 after it became a republic and it became clear that there was some opposition to its continuing membership.

I agreed that the attorney-general was correct in saying that constitutional status is not a *criterion* of membership. But convention clearly requires that a change of this nature be approved, or at least not opposed by any one of the other 53 governments. No Republic–ACM has always believed that all of the consequences of change, legal, political and financial be placed before the people. They are all entitled to be in a position to cast an informed vote.

The ARM then issued a press release on 13 May under this heading: "Australians for Constitutional Monarchy talk nonsense about Australia's membership of the commonwealth."

My warning was dismissed as "silly", "an insult to the intelligence of all Australians" and "shameful". In what one journalist described as a "battle of press releases", I then asked, "Why not check the facts on commonwealth membership?"

I pointed out ACM had never claimed that we would be excluded from the commonwealth if we were to become a republic.

In the meantime, I had decided it was time to lay this *canard* to rest. So I wrote to the secretary-general of the commonwealth, Chief Emeka Anyaoku. His Excellency replied on 18 May 1999. The commonwealth secretariat approved my releasing his letter, provided the text were published in full. It reads:

Thank you for your letter of 11 May 1999 which I saw on my return from overseas travel.

You are right in your understanding of the procedures within the Commonwealth when a country changes its constitutional status to that of a republic. On being notified of the change by the government concerned and in the light of an express wish to continue Commonwealth membership, I would then contact all other Commonwealth countries seeking their concurrence for the change. In the normal course of events, this process is not more than a formality, and was most recently followed when Mauritius became a republic on 12 March 1992.

When I released this I pointed out that I said that any other treatment of any such Australian application would be outrageous and should be condemned by all Australians.

It is conceivable that were Australia's continuing membership of the commonwealth in issue, dissatisfied groups in Australia might lobby other commonwealth members. They already do so in other international bodies. They could argue that our policies were in breach of commonwealth principles. What would happen is impossible to predict. Let us hope any change did not coincide with similar diplomatic incidents to those where an Australian prime minister once called a commonwealth prime minister "recalcitrant" or its legal procedures "barbaric", as happened under two previous governments!

Our presence in the important forum for European-Asia economic issues, ASEM, is already denied by the veto of just one country. The last summit, held in London on 3–4 April 1998, was chaired by Tony Blair, United Kingdom prime minister and then president of the European Union Council. It brought together the 15 European Union States, the European Union Commission, the seven ASEAN countries (Brunei, Indonesia, Malaysia, Philippines, Singapore, Thailand and Vietnam), as well as the People's Republic of China, Japan and Korea.

It was an important meeting; the second in a series. Australia wanted to be there and should have been there. Our presence was desired by all the other 25 states – except one. We were vetoed. Lest it be thought this is of no importance, the summit itself confirmed the importance of the Europe-Asia partnership. It approved a number of initiatives taken since the first summit in Bangkok. And it laid the foundations for ASEM's future development. Two separate statements were adopted, one of which concerned the financial and economic crisis affecting several Asian countries.

The statement on the crisis in Asia stressed the parties' interest in restoring economic stability and the need for swift implementation of reforms in the countries affected. The European Union and the Asian countries expressed their support for strengthening the monetary system, which entailed stepping up the supervisory role of the IMF and increasing the available quotas. They undertook jointly to combat protectionist reactions and continue the effort towards multilateral liberalisation by maintaining investment flows to Asia. They also reiterated their concern at the social impact of the crisis, stating that it was necessary to safeguard social expenditure as far as possible. The Europeans agreed to finance technical assistance to Asian countries in the financial and social fields, to which the Commission was to contribute ECU 15 million. It agreed to the creation of a European network of financial experts to facilitate financial reform and enable the countries of Asia to benefit from European know-how in this field.

The final overall statement covered the development of political dialogue on important regional issues such as Cambodia, Korea, and the EU enlargement. In the economic sphere, it affirmed the need for measures to promote investment and trade implemented since the Bangkok Summit, for setting clear objectives for the next summit in the year 2000, and for continuing the dialogue on multilateral trade questions. Global and cultural issues were also broached, notably in initiatives to combat the sexual exploitation of children, discussions on the environment and international crime and proposals in the social and cultural field. Parallel to the creation of a "vision group" charged with examining the long-term prospects for relations between Asia and Europe, a Euro-Asia framework of cooperation was put in place, stressing the priorities for the future and highlighting the three pillars of such cooperation; high-level political dialogue, economic cooperation and the strengthening of mutual understanding.

All of these issues were of great and continuing concern to Australia. We should have had an input. And would have, but for one country's veto. Malaysia decided that we should not be there.

In recent years Australia has been disappointed in some of its plans for our role in international forums – quite often after the holding out by well-known ARM supporters that we would be successful. One was in relation to the secretary-generalship of the commonwealth itself, the other our candidature for a seat on the security council.

The ARM and its supporters are well aware that Australia

does not have the enormous resources of other countries (and groups of countries) to buy international influence. Nor does it have superpower clout. As an old western democracy – actually multiracial, tolerant and welcoming – it is too frequently portrayed as insular, intolerant and racist, even by elements within Australia. It is an easier target for international busybodies than those countries with authoritarian governments, indifferent to human rights, where an increasingly intolerant monoculturalism prevails.

Our membership of the commonwealth is precious. It is a club in which we play – and have since its foundation always played – a significant role with countries which are particularly close to us. It allows us to compete in the Commonwealth Games.

The point is that rather than denying the existence of the documented commonwealth convention that when a realm becomes a republic all other members must agree to its continuing membership, the ARM should be investigating how best to ensure this agreement. After all, it is the ARM that is proposing change. The onus is on the proponents of such change both to demonstrate and assure Australians that it will be as simple as they claim and that there will be no unexpected results.

POSTSCRIPT

Why has Australia, and not say, Argentina, such an enviable record in stable, democratic government? Why was Australia able to play such a significant role in the world, and to prosper, and not Argentina? In 1901 the people of Australia and Argentina were among the world's richest. Argentina is no longer.

Surely our constitutional system, in the broadest sense, provides much of the answer.

This allowed us to be given our independence, not to fight for it. It allowed us to evolve into self-governing communities and to federate. All of this was achieved by peaceful evolution, not sudden revolutionary change.

The movement of federation was expedited by the Corowa plan in 1893. That presupposed the people's involvement and approval at every stage. In contrast the Keating–Turnbull process which began 100 years later, essentially involved republican elites deciding great issues in private, among themselves.

This has culminated in the second Keating–Turnbull republic, a model which was scrambled together in the very last days of the 1998 Constitutional Convention. The result of deals and trade-offs behind the scenes, it was designed to secure the maximum vote on the floor. It was designed neither to achieve the checks and balances a democracy must have, nor to transfer power to the people. It was so hastily conceived that the bill giving it effect was amended several times in its last hours in the parliament.

Its worst feature is not that the president is to be chosen by back room deals and trade-offs between the politicians. The worst feature is that the president, who is surely there to protect the constitutional process from subversion, is to hold office at the whim of the prime minister.

That this would be the central feature of the so-called republic was never disclosed in the convention elections. It did not even see the light of day until near the end of the convention.

No other nation has ever adopted such a republic. Because, as Harry Evans rightly observes, no other nation has been so mis-guided as to adopt such a model.

It is a fact beyond dispute that every so often a political system, however democratic, will throw up a rogue. Someone who is desperate for power – either to attain it, keep it, or magnify it. Someone who is prepared to break the conventions, the laws and even the constitution to achieve his or her ends.

A principal purpose of a constitution is to ensure, through checks and balances, that this just cannot happen.

The awesome truth about the ill-considered proposal on which the people are to vote is that, rather than thwarting such a rogue or even a band of rogues, it will actually ease their path.

As former Chief Justice Sir Harry Gibbs warned: "Not even a committed republican, who spent a few minutes pondering this model, and who cares for the future of this country, could possibly vote for it."

BIBLIOGRAPHY

Abbott, A., *The Minimal Monarchy*, Adelaide, Wakefield Press, 1995

Arnold, Spearitt & Walker (eds), *Out of Empire*, Mandarin Australia, 1993

Andres, Christopher, *Secret Intelligence and the American Presidency*, Harper Collins, 1995

Armaud de Maurepas, Hervé Robert, Peirre Thibault, *Les Grands Hommes d'Etat de L'Histoire de France*, Paris, Larousse, 1989

Atkinson, A, *The Muddle Headed Republic*, Melbourne, Oxford University Press, 1993

Australia Constitutional Commission, Final Report of the Constitutional Commission 1988, Canberra: AGPS, 1998

Australia Constitutional Convention (1998) *Report of the Constitutional Convention*, Old Parliament House, Canberra, 2–13 February 1998

Australian National Flag Association, Video Kit

Australian National Flag Association. Website: www.flagaustnat.asn

Australian Republican Movement Platform. Website: www.republic. org.au/arm/platform.html

Bogdanor, V., & Marshall, G., "Dismissing Governors-General", *Public Law*, 1996, pp 205–13

Bogdanor, V., *The Monarchy and the Constitution*, London, Clarendon Press, 1995

Bradford, S., *Elizabeth, A Bibliography of Her Majesty the Queen*, London, Heinemann, 1996

Commonwealth Government Directory, December 1995–February, 1996

Constitution Papers, see Parliamentary Research Service

Daly, F., *From Curtin to Kerr*, Melbourne: Sun Books, 1997

Dixon, O., The "Law and the Constitution" (1935) 51 Law Quarterly Review 590

Evatt, H.V., *The King and his Dominion Governors*, 2nd edn, London, Franck Cass and Co. Ltd, 1967

Farthing, J., *Freedom Wears a Crown*, Toronto 1957

Forsey, E., "Crown and Cabinet", in *Collected Essays Freedom and Order*, Toronto, McCelland and Stewart Ltd, 1974

Forsey, E., *Freedom and Order*, Toronto, McClelland and Stewart Ltd, 1974

Frost, D., *Whitlam and Frost*, London, Sundial Publications Ltd, 1974

Galligan, B., *A Federal Republic*, Melbourne, Cambridge University Press, 1995

Grainger & Jones (eds), *The Australian Constitutional Monarchy*, Sydney, ACM Publishing, 1994

Hamilton, J. Madison and Jacy, J. – *The Federalist*, 1787, 1979 edn, Norwalk, The Eastern Press, 1979

Handley, K.R. and Holloway, Ian, *Lessons from Commonwealth Countries*, Sydney, ACM Publishing, 1998

Heard, A., *Canadian Constitutional Conventions*, Toronto, Oxford University Press, 1991

Hirst, J., *A Republican Manifesto*, Melbourne, Oxford University Press, 1994

Horne, D., *The Coming Republic*, Sydney, Pan MacMillan, 1992

Howard, C., *Australian Federal Constitutional Law*, 3rd edn, Sydney, Law Book Co., 1985

Hughes, R., *Culture of Complaints*, New York, Oxford University Press, 1993

Johnson, Paul, *A History of the American People*, London, Weidenfield and Nicolson, 1997

Keating, P.J., *An Australian Republic: The Way Forward*, speech by the prime minister 7 June 1995, Canberra, published by AGPS, 1995

Kelly, Paul, *The Age of Certainty*, St Leonards, Allen and Unwin, Rev. edn, 1994

Keneally, T., *Our Republic*, Port Melbourne, Heinemann 1993

Kerr, J., *Matters for Judgement*, Melbourne, MacMillan, 1988

Kirby M.D., "A Republic by Stealth?", Robert Harris Oration, 12th Convention of the Royal Australasian College of Dental Surgeons, Canberra, 16 April 1993

Kramer, L., address given at Launch of ACM, Sydney Town Hall, 4 June 1993

Lane, P.H., *An Introduction to the Australian Constitutions*, 6th edn, Sydney, The Law Book Co., 1994

Landes, D., in *The Wealth and Poverty of Nations*, Little Brown, London: W. W. Norton, 1998

Lazar D., *The Frozen Republic*, New York, Harcourt Brace, 1996

Lindell, G.J., "Why is Australia's Constitution Binding? – The Reasons in 1900 and now, and the effect of Independence", *Federal Law Review*, Vol 16, 1986, pp 29–49

Maddox G., *Australian Democracy in Theory and Practice*, 3rd edn, Melbourne, Longman, 1996

Marshall, G., *Constitutional Conventions*, Oxford University Press, 1984

Mason, Sir Anthony, "Constitutional issues Relating to the Republic as They Affect the States", address given to the Constitutional Centenary Foundation, Parliament House, Sydney, 27 May 1998

Mason, Sir Anthony, "The Republic and Australian Constitutional Development" (not a published title), Seminar, Australian National University, 11 May 1998

McDonald, T., *The Queen and the Commonwealth*, Thames Methcien, London, 1986

McKenna, M., *The Captive Republic*, Cambridge, Cambridge University Press, 1996

Menzies, R.G., *Afternoon Light*, Melbourne, Cassell, 1967

Minogue, K., *Citizenship and Monarchy*, London, Institute of United States Studies, University of London, 1998)

O'Brien, P., *The People's Case*, Collingwood, Australian Scholarly Publishing, 1995

O'Connell, D.P., "Canada, Australia Constitutional Reform and the Crown", *The Parliamentarian*, 1983, Vol. LX No. 1, 5–13, 8

O'Keefe, B., *Australia 1998: An Independent & Self-Determining Nation*, Sydney, ACM Publishing, 1998

Official Report, *National Australasian Convention Debates*, 2 March to 9 April 1891

Olfield, Audrey, *The Great Republic of the Southern Seas*, Sydney, Hale & Iremonger, 1999

Parliamentary Research Service, *The Constitution Papers*, Subject Collection No. 7, Canberra, AGPS, 1996

Patmore, G.A. and Whyte, J.D., "Imaging Constitutional Crisis: Power and (mis)behaviour in Republican Australia", 25 *Federal Law Review*, 1997, 181

Quick, J., and Garran, R., *The Annotated Constitution of the Australian Commonwealth*, Sydney, Angus and Robertson, 1901

Republic Advisory Committee, *An Australian Republic: The Options*, AGPS, Canberra, 1993, Vol I, II

Sampford, C., and Wood, D., *Codification of Constitutional Conventions in Australia*, *Public Law*, 1987, 231

Sharma, Indra, *Modern Constitutions at Work*, London, Asia Publishing House, 1962

Smith, D., *Reflections of a Constitutional Convention Delegate*, address given 27 March 1998, published by the Australian Monarchist League, Double Bay, 1998

Smith, D., *The Role of the Governor-General; our Australian Head of State*, Sydney, ACM Publishing, 1997

Smith, D., "A Funny Thing Happened on the Way to the Forum", *Upholding the Australian Constitution*, *The Samuel Griffith Society*, Vol 10, 1–48, August, 1998

Smith, Stephen Murray, edn, *The Dictionary of Australian Quotations*, Port Melbourne, Mandarin, 1992

Stephenson, M.A. and Turner, C. (eds), *Australia Republic or Monarchy?*, St Lucia, University of Queensland Press, 1994

The Australian Constitution: Essential Documents in Australian Constitutional History, Sydney, ACM Publishing, 1997

University of NSW Law Journal Forum, Vol. 4 No. 2, June 1998

Thompson, P., *Kava in the Blood*, Auckland, Tandem, 1999

Turnbull, M., *The Reluctant Republic*, Port Melbourne, Heinemann, 1993

Whitlam G., *The Truth of the Matter*, Melbourne, Penguin, 1979

Williams, G., "The High Court and the People", in Selby, H., (ed) *Tomorrow's Law*, Leichhardt, NSW, Federation Press, 1995

Ziegler, P., *King Edward VIII*, London, Collins, 1990

Wakefield Press has been publishing good Australian books
for over fifty years. For a catalogue of current and
forthcoming titles, or to add your name to our mailing list,
send your name and address to

Wakefield Press, Box 2266, Kent Town, South Australia 5071.

TELEPHONE (08) 8362 8800 FAX (08) 8362 7592
WEB www.wakefieldpress.com.au

A R T S A

Wakefield Press thanks Wirra Wirra Vineyards and
Arts South Australia for their continued support.